Discovering Fiction

A READER OF NORTH AMERICAN SHORT STORIES

AN INTRODUCTION

2nd Edition

Judith Kay
Rosemary Gelshenen

CAMBRIDGE
UNIVERSITY PRESS

CAMBRIDGE
UNIVERSITY PRESS

University Printing House, Cambridge CB2 8BS, United Kingdom

One Liberty Plaza, 20th Floor, New York, NY 10006, USA

477 Williamstown Road, Port Melbourne, VIC 3207, Australia

314–321, 3rd Floor, Plot 3, Splendor Forum, Jasola District Centre, New Delhi – 110025, India

79 Anson Road, #06–04/06, Singapore 079906

Cambridge University Press is part of the University of Cambridge.

It furthers the University's mission by disseminating knowledge in the pursuit of education, learning and research at the highest international levels of excellence.

www.cambridge.org
Information on this title: www.cambridge.org/9781107638020

© Cambridge University Press 2013

First Edition first published 2001
Second Edition published 2013
Reprinted 2019

Printed in Italy by Rotolito S.p.A.

A catalogue record for this publication is available from the British Library

ISBN 978-1-107-63802-0 Student's Book Introduction
ISBN 555-5-559-33268-0 Instructor's Manual Introduction
ISBN 978-1-107-65222-4 Student's Book 1
ISBN 555-5-559-21768-0 Instructor's Manual 1
ISBN 978-1-107-62214-2 Student's Book 2
ISBN 555-5-559-03087-6 Instructor's Manual 2

Art direction, book design, editorial management, and layout services: Hyphen S.A.
Cover images: Dougal Waters/Media Bakery
Illustrations: Dan Brown: *The Californian's Tale, The Tree of Knowledge;* Alicia Hough: *A Pair of Silk Stockings, The Pace of Youth;* Rob Lawson: *Young Man Axelbrod, Its Wavering Image;* Victor Moschopoulos: *Omit Flowers, Rain, Rain Go Away;* Tim Otis: *One Thousand Dollars, All the Years of Her Life;* Ruth Palmer: *David Swan, The Legend of Sleepy Hollow.*

CONTENTS

HIGHLIGHTS

CHAPTER 1

Young Man Axelbrod
SINCLAIR LEWIS

A PREPARING TO READ

1 Think Before You Read

Answer the following questions:

1 Why do people go to college?
2 What should someone do to prepare for college?
3 What are the qualities of a good college student?
4 How do you feel when you have a much older student in one of your classes?

2 Picture Focus

With a partner, talk about the picture. Who are the two men? Where are they going?

4 Making Choices

THINK BEFORE YOU READ

Reflecting on the topic before reading helps students connect to the story.

---

5 Making Predictions

From the Story Preview, try to predict what will happen. Circle one choice below or write your own answer. Discuss your prediction with a partner.

What will Knute do at the university?

1 He will study hard and be better than the younger students.
2 He will leave the university and go back home.
3 He will go to a different university.
4 _____

6 Idioms and Expressions

You will find these idioms and expressions in the story:

sun went down sunset; time just before darkness	**don't fit in** be different from other people; not belong
pass an examination do well on a test	**get there in plenty of time** arrive very early
boarded a train got on a train	**walk arm in arm** walk with one arm hooked around another person's arm
lose its magic not be as exciting as it was before; become disappointing	**get tired of** become bored with something; become impatient with something

7 Literary Term: Setting

The **setting** is the time and place of the story. This story begins on a farm in Minnesota and ends in a university town in Connecticut. The setting changes from a peaceful landscape in the Midwest to a northeastern college town where young people from many different places come to study.

Focus As you read the story, notice how Knute's experiences change as the setting changes and how Knute feels with each experience.

6 Making Choices

IDIOMS AND EXPRESSIONS

A special focus on the meanings of idioms and expressions prepares students for reading literature.

LITERARY TERM

Important literary terms are presented, preparing students to read fiction beyond the classroom.

ABOUT THE AUTHOR

Biographical information introduces students to some of the most influential writers in North American fiction, giving context to the stories.

THE STORY

Adapted short stories depict a variety of experiences, helping students deepen their understanding of North American culture.

READING COMPREHENSION

Comprehension questions scaffold students' understanding of the story.

GUESSING MEANING FROM CONTEXT

After each story, students guess the meaning of unknown words – one of the most important skills for independent reading.

3 Grammar: Adverbs

Adverbs are words that modify (describe, change, or add information to) action verbs, adjectives, and other adverbs. Adverbs also answer the questions of *where, when, how, how much*.

● Adverbs modify verbs. In the following sentence from the story, *seriously* is an adverb because it modifies the verb *repeated*. The adverb here answers the question *how*.

"One thousand dollars," repeated Lawyer Tolman, seriously . . .

● Adverbs modify adjectives. In this sentence from the story, *too* modifies the adjective *little*. The adverb here answers the question *how much*.

"It's . . . too little to invest."

● Adverbs modify other adverbs. In this sentence from the story, *very* modifies the adverb *much*.

"I thank you very much, Sir."

● You will find that many adverbs add *-ly* to the adjective form. However, not all words that end in *-ly* are adverbs. In this sentence from the story, *unfriendly* is an adjective (not an adverb) that modifies *way*.

Mr. Tolman looked at him in an unfriendly way.

● Some adverbs do not have an adjective form. Examples are *just, always, then, again, soon, not, very*, and *never*.

Application 1   In each of the following sentences from the story, there is at least one adverb. Find the adverb and underline it. Then in the space on the right, write the word the adverb modifies.

1 "I'll do my best," said the young man politely.   *said*

2 "I just came from my deceased uncle's company."   _____

3 "You've always had plenty of money to spend."   _____

GRAMMAR

Students improve their reading comprehension by reviewing a grammar point modeled in the story.

D   THINKING CRITICALLY

1 Discussing the Story

With a partner or in a small group, discuss the following questions:

1 Why doesn't Miss Hayden return Gillian's love?
2 Does Gillian really love Miss Hayden, or does he love Miss Lauriere?
3 What would happen if Gillian did not tear up his note?
4 What do you think Miss Hayden will do with the money?
5 What would you do if you were Gillian?

2 Making Inferences

Authors often write something that can have more than one meaning. You need to figure out what the author means. This is called making inferences. Read the following sentences from the story. Then circle the answer that shows the author's meaning. If you need help, look back at the story. Discuss your answers.

1 ". . . and that's where the joke comes in. He left his whole fortune to science."
   a Gillian thinks his uncle was a funny man.
   b Gillian can't believe his uncle left all his money only to science.
   c Gillian is telling his friend a lie.

2 Gillian said, "Was Miss Hayden left anything in my uncle's will besides $10?"
   a Gillian is thinking of giving his money to Miss Hayden.
   b Gillian wants Miss Hayden's money.
   c Gillian wants to know if Miss Hayden got his uncle's house.

3 "I've just come from Tolman's office. They've been looking at some papers and found that my uncle left you a thousand dollars. Here it is."
   a Gillian wants Miss Hayden to have the one thousand dollars.
   b Gillian is joking with Miss Hayden.
   c Gillian is telling Miss Hayden that the lawyers made a mistake.

MAKING INFERENCES

Students practice making inferences, an important critical thinking skill in every academic discipline.

3 Analyzing the Story: Tone

As you read on page 156, tone shows the writer's feelings about the subject and characters. The writer sets the tone through description and dialogue. Three types of tone from the story are in the chart. Examples of descriptions or dialogue are shown for each type of tone. Read the story again and look for more examples to add to the chart.

TONE
of "All the Years of Her Life"

NERVOUSNESS	SILENCE	ANGER
"What things? What are you talking about?"	*Mrs. Higgins took long steps, and her serious face looked worried.*	*"Be quiet. Don't speak to me. You've disgraced me again and again."*

4 Summarizing

Put the following sentences in the correct order to summarize the story. Write the numbers 1 to 6 to show the order. The first one has been done for you.

____ Mr. Carr calls Mrs. Higgins on the telephone.

____ Alfred and his mother walk home in silence.

_1_ Mr. Carr accuses Alfred of stealing from the store.

____ Mrs. Higgins is calm and dignified in the store.

____ Mr. Carr agrees not to call the police.

____ Alfred watches his mother drink the tea with a trembling hand.

5 Writing

Pretend you are Alfred. Write a letter to Mr. Carr. Explain how sorry you are about stealing from him and about the lesson you learned.

ANALYZING THE STORY

Students refine their understanding of the literary term in a close reading of the story facilitated by a graphic organizer.

WRITING

A variety of writing assignments mirror response writing students will encounter in college.

C ELEMENTS OF A SHORT STORY

Filling Out the Elements Chart

This chart shows the five basic elements of a short story. You can find definitions for these elements on page 170. Some of these elements have been filled out for "Young Man Axelbrod." Complete the chart. Then copy the blank chart on page xvi and fill it out for "A Pair of Silk Stockings" or "One Thousand Dollars" or for both stories. Share your charts with a partner or in a small group.

Elements of _____*Young Man Axelbrod*_____
(name of story)

SETTING

CHARACTERS

PLOT
Knute Axelbrod is a retired farmer who wants to be a scholar. He gets accepted at Yale University. At Yale he becomes lonely and disappointed. Then he meets Gil Washburn. One night they walk in the moonlight and discuss great men and their ideas. Gil reads a book of French poetry and then gives it to Knute. Knute is content, but the next morning he decides to return home.

CONFLICT
The conflict is between Knute's desire to become a serious student and the difficulty he faces because he is no longer young and is different from the other students.

THEME(s)
Sometimes our dreams and plans don't happen the way we want them to. One wonderful experience can make up for many disappointments.

WEBQUEST

Find more information about the topics in Part One by going on the Internet. Go to www.cambridge.org/discoveringfiction/wq and follow the instructions for doing a WebQuest. Have fun. Enjoy the quest!

WEBQUEST

Engaging WebQuests send students to authentic websites, building their confidence, fluency, and ability to read across different media.

Elements of a Short Story Chart

Name _____ Date _____

Choose a story to analyze and write its name on the blank line in the chart. Then complete the chart with a few sentences for each of the elements: *setting, characters, plot, conflict,* and *theme(s)*.

Elements of _____

(name of story)

SETTING

CHARACTERS

PLOT

CONFLICT

THEME(S)

Discovering Fiction

A Reader of North American Short Stories

AN INTRODUCTION

PART ONE

Making Choices

EVERY DAY, we make choices about what to do which can affect our lives. Some choices we make are small, such as what to eat, what to wear, or what to do that day. Other choices we make are big and can lead to our success or failure, our happiness, or disappointment. Characters in literature, as in real life, also have to make choices.

In the three stories you are about to read, an elderly man chooses what to do after he retires, a housewife chooses how she will spend some money she has saved, and a young man chooses what to do with $1,000 from his uncle. As you read these stories, ask yourself if you agree with the choices the characters make. What choices would you make if you were the three characters?

Young Man Axelbrod

SINCLAIR LEWIS

A PREPARING TO READ

1 Think Before You Read

Answer the following questions:

1 Why do people go to college?
2 What should someone do to prepare for college?
3 What are the qualities of a good college student?
4 How do you feel when you have a much older student in one of your classes?

2 Picture Focus

With a partner, talk about the picture. Who are the two men? Where are they going?

3 Words to Know

Study the following key words from the story. They all relate to *going to college*. Then complete the paragraph using each word once.

scholar a person who studies and loves learning; a person who has a lot of knowledge	**grades** scores from a test or a course, using the letters A, B, C, D, or F
knowledge information that someone receives from experience or studying	**literature** books, stories, poems, plays, etc., with artistic value
degree a title given by a college or university for completing a program of courses	**assignments** work or study that you must do for a class

There are many students who go to a college or university just to get a

_____. But a true _____ is someone who studies

because he or she has a love of learning. Perhaps such students study

_____ so that they can gain _____ from the words

of great writers and poets. And when they do their _____, they

are not worried about the _____ that the teacher gives them.

They study because they love learning something new.

4 Story Preview

Read the preview of the story. Then answer the question in Making Predictions on the next page.

Knute Axelbrod is a retired farmer who decides to go to college. He is accepted at Yale University. He is excited about studying at a big university, but his love of knowledge is not enough to make him happy. The other students think he is old and strange. He becomes very lonely and disappointed and misses his farm and family.

5 Making Predictions

From the Story Preview, try to predict what will happen. Circle one choice below or write your own answer. Discuss your prediction with a partner.

What will Knute do at the university?

1 He will study hard and be better than the younger students.

2 He will leave the university and go back home.

3 He will go to a different university.

4 _____

6 Idioms and Expressions

You will find these idioms and expressions in the story:

sun went down sunset; time just before darkness	**don't fit in** be different from other people; not belong
pass an examination do well on a test	**get there in plenty of time** arrive very early
boarded a train got on a train	**walk arm in arm** walk with one arm hooked around another person's arm
lose its magic not be as exciting as it was before; become disappointing	**get tired of** become bored with something; become impatient with something

7 Literary Term: Setting

The **setting** is the time and place of the story. This story begins on a farm in Minnesota and ends in a university town in Connecticut. The setting changes from a peaceful landscape in the Midwest to a northeastern college town where young people from many different places come to study.

Focus   As you read the story, notice how Knute's experiences change as the setting changes and how Knute feels with each experience.

About the Author

Sinclair Lewis (1885–1951), a novelist, short-story writer, and playwright, was born in Sauk Center, Minnesota. His father was a country doctor, and Sinclair often helped him when he went to visit his patients. One of his most famous novels was *Arrowsmith*, which has a country doctor as its main character.

Sinclair Lewis went to Yale University. He was a sailor, and he went to Panama to help build the Panama Canal. He had various jobs as a reporter, editor, lecturer, and writer. He published several popular novels including *Babbitt* and *Main Street*. In 1930, he became the first American to receive the Nobel Prize for Literature.

Young Man Axelbrod

Knute Axelbrod was born in Scandinavia. As a young man he dreamed of being a famous scholar. When he first came to America, he worked all day and studied all evening. He even taught school for a short time. After he married, he gave up teaching and reading and became a farmer.
5   He had a wife and three children, and he no longer had the free time to read the books he loved.

Knute worked hard for many years. Then one day, when he was sixty-five, he realized he was an old man. His wife was dead, and his children were grown up. His two sons lived in other states, and Knute decided to
10 give the farm to his daughter Angela and her husband. He built himself a small house nearby and spent his days in the garden growing vegetables and flowers.

After Knute gave his daughter his farm, he still had the habits of a farmer. He awoke at five every morning, cleaned his house, made his
15 bed, and worked in the garden. He was in bed by the time the sun went down. Soon, he began changing his habits. He slept until seven or eight in the mornings, and he often took long walks at night. The neighbors began to talk about Knute. They thought his night walks were strange.

He bought a cat and named her Princess. He let her drink milk from a
bowl on the kitchen table. He talked to her as if she were human.

Knute often sat in the sun and looked at the trees. His wide shoulders
leaned against his rocking chair, and he touched his white beard. One
day while he was sitting in his chair on the porch, he looked up at the
trees and thought, "I'm an old man. I've had a good life, but there's
one thing I wish for in my old age. I want to go to college. I want to be
a student again and read all the great books I never had time to read."

Knute always had a young soul that looked for knowledge and beauty.
He loved learning and thought that all college students loved to study
and learn. He pictured Harvard and Yale as famous universities where
students, like the ancient Greeks, stood around under marble temples[1]
and talked about great ideas. He ordered college catalogs and textbooks.
He studied Latin, algebra, English, and history. He studied twelve hours
a day, and all this time he kept it a secret. Finally, one day he told his
daughter.

"I just want you to know that I'm going to college. I plan to leave
next week."

"Father, what are you talking about? You can't go to college. You're
too old."

"I'm leaving in a few days. I'm not too old to keep learning. I've been
studying, and I think I can pass the examinations."

"But the other students are eighteen or nineteen years old."

"That's not a problem. I don't have to go dancing with them. I just
want to be in college with them."

"What if you get sick?"

"Angela, I'm not a child. If I get sick, I'll go to a doctor. Don't worry,
my dear. I'll be all right."

Angela realized that her father was not going to listen to her. "Dad,
where are you planning to go to school?"

"Yale. I'm going to Yale."

The next day he brought Princess over to his daughter's house along
with some of his plants. His daughter agreed to watch his little house.
Knute said goodbye and boarded a train to New Haven, Connecticut. He
had to travel across the United States from his home in Minnesota.

Knute Axelbrod passed the entrance examinations and was accepted
at Yale. His roommate was Ray Gribble. Ray was a teacher and wanted
a degree so he could make more money. He was surprised that Knute
was interested in studying literature and that he didn't care about
making money.

Knute knew people at Yale thought he was strange. He listened to
instructors who were younger than his sons, and his large body looked

---

[1]**marble temples**: buildings used for religion or education and made of hard stone

uncomfortable in the chairs in the classrooms. Most of the students stared at him and thought he was crazy. Soon, even Gribble, his roommate, stayed away from him.

Yale began to lose its magic for Knute. The buildings were no longer marble temples. The dining room where Knute ate his meals became a lonely place. No one sat next to him or talked to him. Several young men laughed at Knute's beard, and eventually, he began eating at a nearby restaurant. Without friends, it became harder for Knute to do his assignments. Loneliness became his friend. He missed his cat, his daughter, and his little house. He missed the walks at night and the sunshine on his porch. He had been at Yale only a month.

One day Knute climbed a large rock that overlooked the school and saw a young man sitting on a bench. It was Gil Washburn, another freshman. He was a quiet type and not very popular with the other students. Knute stared at him. The young man looked lonely, too.

Gil noticed Knute and walked over to him. "Great view," he said smiling. Knute smiled back and said, "Yes, I think The Acropolis² must be like this."

"You know, Knute, I've been thinking about you. We are the two who don't fit in here. We came to dream, and everyone else is here to get good grades and make money. You may not agree with me, but I think we're very much alike."

"Why do you think I came here to dream?"

"I listen to you talking in class. I watch you with the other students. Do you like poetry? I have a book I brought with me. Do you want to look at it?"

Knute took the thin, brown leather book in his big hands and touched it gently. The pages had gold on their edges. When he opened the pages, he saw a foreign language. "It's beautiful, but I can't read it."

"It's French poetry. Let me read you a little."

---

²**The Acropolis**: a rocky hill in the center of the city of Athens in Greece

Gil read to Knute, and the words sounded like music. Knute had been waiting for this for sixty-five years. Then Gil said, "Listen, there's a concert in Hartford tonight, and Ysaye, a famous violinist, is playing.
105 Let's go hear him. We'll take the train and get there in plenty of time. I asked some of the other fellows, but they thought I was crazy."

Knute never heard of Ysaye, but he said, "Sure." When they got to Hartford, they found out they had just enough money to eat dinner, buy concert tickets, and pay for a train ticket to a nearby town. After the
110 concert, Gil suggested, "Let's walk back to New Haven. Can you walk that far?" Knute had no idea how far away they were, but once again he said, "Sure."

So the young man and the older one walked beneath the October moon. They stopped to steal apples and stare at the moon. Gil did most
115 of the talking, and Knute listened. They reached the campus at five in the morning. Knute didn't know how to thank Gil, so he said, "It was fine. I'll go to bed now and dream about our adventure."

"You can't go to bed now. The fun isn't over. Let's go get something to eat. I'm hungry. I'll go up to my room and get some money. Wait
120 here."

Knute was delighted. He would have waited all night. He had lived sixty-five years and traveled fifteen hundred miles to find Gil Washburn. When Gil returned, the two walked arm in arm down the empty streets until they found a restaurant. For the first time, Knute
125 felt content and happy.

They brought the food up to Gil's room. Knute sat in a comfortable chair and looked around at the books, Persian rugs, a silver tea set, and paintings. Gil started a fire in the small fireplace. As they ate, they spoke about great men and their ideas. Gil read some of his own poetry. Knute
130 thought it was a miracle to meet someone who wrote poetry.

They began to yawn, and Knute said goodbye. As he left Gil's room, he saw the sun coming up. It was a new day.

"I can go to his room anytime now. He's my friend."

Knute held the book of French poetry, which Gil wanted him to keep.
135 As he walked back to his own room, Knute felt very tired. In daylight, the adventure seemed hard to believe.

"Age and youth – I guess they can't be a team for long. If I saw the boy again, he would get tired of me. I told him all I know. This is what I came to college for. I waited sixty-five years for this one night. If I go
140 away now, I won't spoil it."

He wrote a note to Gil and packed his clothes. At five that afternoon, on a westbound train, an old man sat smiling. His eyes were content, and his hands held a small book of French poetry even though he couldn't read French.

C UNDERSTANDING THE STORY

1 Reading Comprehension

With a partner or in a small group, discuss the following questions:

1 Why didn't Knute go to college when he was a young man?
2 How does Knute prepare for the entrance examinations?
3 Why does Knute feel lonely?
4 Why does Knute enjoy being with Gil Washburn?
5 Why does Knute decide to leave Yale and return home?

2 Guessing Meaning from Context

The words in the list are in the story. Find the words in the story and try to understand their meanings. Then complete the sentences with words in the list. Use each word only once.

dream	soul	steal	yawn
realizes	secret	adventure	spoil
habits	stare	content	strange

1 Knute keeps his plan to go to college a _____*secret*_____ from
   his daughter.

2 Angela _____ her father won't give up his plan to go
   to college.

3 The other students at Yale _____ at Knute's white beard.

4 They think Knute is _____.

5 When he leaves his farm in Minnesota, Knute starts a new

   _____ .

6 Knute has a _____ of going to college and studying literature.

7 After Knute gives his farm to his daughter, he still has the

   _____ of a farmer.

8 Knute and Gil stop to _____ apples from a tree on their walk back to Yale.

9 Knute and Gil both _____ because they are sleepy after staying up all night.

10 After spending time with Gil Washburn, Knute feels _____.

11 Knute wants to leave college so that he doesn't _____ his friendship with Gil.

12 Knute has the _____ of a scholar because he loves learning.

3 Grammar: Proper and Common Nouns

Nouns are words for people, places, or things. Most nouns are either proper nouns or common nouns.

● Proper nouns are for specific people, places, or things. In English, proper nouns begin with a capital letter.

Specific people, places, and things include:

names, countries, cities, states, schools, buildings, streets, rivers, lakes, oceans, nationalities, languages, religions, holidays, months, days, and titles

Examples:

Knute Axelbrod	America	Greek
Angela	England	English
Professor Smith	Minnesota	October
Yale University	The Acropolis	Sunday

● Common nouns are not specific people, places, or things. They do not begin with a capital letter.

Examples:

farmer	garden	flowers
roommate	campus	poetry
friend	temples	concert

Application 1 In the following sentences, some proper nouns are missing. With a partner, fill in the blank lines with correct proper nouns from the story. Capitalize the first letter of each proper noun.

1 Knute Axelbrod was born in ___*Scandinavia*___ and later came to

  ___*America*___ .

2 Knute had a cat named _____ .

3 _____ and _____ are famous centers of learning.

4 To prepare for college, Knute studied _____ , algebra,

  _____ , and history.

5 _____ realized that her father was not going to listen to her.

6 Knute traveled by train from _____ to _____

  _____ , _____ .

7 When Knute saw the view from the large rock, he said, "Yes, I think The

  _____ must be like this."

8 Knute and _____ went to a concert in _____ .

9 After the concert, they walked back under the _____ moon.

10 Gil gave Knute a book of _____ poetry.

Application 2 In the following paragraph, look for the common nouns and proper nouns. Circle the common nouns. Underline the proper nouns. Capitalize the first letter of each proper noun.

K   G   H
knute and gil went to hartford for a concert. They ran out of money and

couldn't take a train back to yale. So they had to walk back to the university.

They stayed up all night talking about great men and their ideas. In the morning,

gil gave knute his book of french poetry. When knute decided to return to

minnesota, he was content with his adventure in connecticut.

D THINKING CRITICALLY

1 Discussing the Story

With a partner or in a small group, discuss the following questions:

1 Why does Knute want to go to college?
2 Why don't the younger students like Knute?
3 Compare Knute and Gil. How are they alike, and how are they different?
4 Did Knute make the right choice in returning to Minnesota? Why or why not?
5 Why do you think the story is titled "Young Man Axelbrod"?

2 Making Inferences

Authors often write something that can have more than one meaning. You need to figure out what the author means. This is called making inferences. Read the following sentences from the story. Then circle the answer that shows the author's meaning. If you need help, look back at the story. Discuss your answers.

1 Knute always had a young soul that looked for knowledge and beauty.
   a Knute was a young man.
   b Knute wanted to keep on learning even though he was older.
   c Knute loved beautiful clothes and jewelry.

2 Most of the students stared at Knute and thought he was crazy.
   a Most students were scared of Knute because he was big.
   b Most students didn't like Knute because he had an unusual name.
   c Most students thought Knute was too old, too big, and too strange.

3 Yale began to lose its magic for Knute.
   a Yale was not the wonderful place Knute thought it would be.
   b Yale didn't teach magic.
   c Knute wanted to become young again.

3 Analyzing the Story: Setting

As you read on page 6, the setting is the time and place of the story. In this story, there are several settings. Knute has different experiences and feelings in each setting. Choose the correct experiences and feelings to complete the chart.

	Experiences		Feelings

Experiences

- The other students don't sit next to Knute or talk to him.
- Knute thinks about his adventures.
- Gil reads his poetry.
- Knute and Gil walk and talk beneath the October moon.

Feelings

- Knute has a good time, but he doesn't know how to thank Gil.
- Knute is content.
- Knute is lonely and disappointed.
- Knute thinks it is a miracle to meet someone who writes poetry.

SETTING	EXPERIENCES	FEELINGS
In the classrooms and dining room at Yale		*Knute is lonely and disappointed.*
On the road from Hartford to New Haven		
In Gil Washburn's room		
On a train to Minnesota	*Knute thinks about his adventures.*	

4 Summarizing

Put the following sentences in the correct order to summarize the story. Write the numbers 1 to 7 to show the order. The first one has been done for you.

____ Knute takes an examination and is accepted at Yale.

____ Gil gives Knute a book of French poetry.

____ Knute feels lonely at school.

____ Knute meets Gil Washburn, who becomes his friend.

_1_ Knute decides to go to college.

____ Knute and Gil go to a concert and stay up all night.

____ Knute decides to return to Minnesota.

5 Writing

Pretend you are Knute. Write a letter to Gil telling him why you left Yale.

CHAPTER 2

A Pair of Silk Stockings

KATE CHOPIN

A PREPARING TO READ

1 Think Before You Read

Answer the following questions:

1 What are the qualities of a good mother? List them.
2 Why do people save money? What things do they usually save their money to buy?
3 Do you like to buy things for yourself or for other people? Explain your answer.

2 Picture Focus

With a partner, talk about the picture. What do you think the woman is thinking about? How do you think she feels?

3 Words to Know

Study the following key words from the story. They all relate to *shopping* and *money*. Then complete the paragraph using each word once.

save keep your money, not spend it	**sale** a time when things in a store are sold at a special low price
wallet something to carry and keep money in	**reduced** at a lower price than is normal
bargain something that is sold at a very good price – much lower than usual	**change** the money you get back when you give more money than the cost of something

Everyone likes to get a _____. When a store has a big _____, a lot of people will come to shop. They will look for things that are _____. It's great to get something for less money than it usually costs. Then you can put the _____ in your _____ and _____ it for another day.

4 Story Preview

Read the preview of the story. Then answer the question in Making Predictions on the next page.

Mrs. Sommers is a housewife in the late 1800s. She is usually very practical. She always saves her money and thinks carefully about how to spend it. One day she goes shopping by herself. She has $15 and plans to buy new clothes for her four children.

5 Making Predictions

From the Story Preview, try to predict what will happen. Circle one choice below or write your own answer. Discuss your prediction with a partner.

What will Mrs. Sommers do when she goes shopping with her $15?

1 She will buy new clothes for her children.

2 She will spend the money on herself.

3 She will save the money and add more money to it.

4 _____

6 Idioms and Expressions

You will find these idioms and expressions in the story:

watched every penny spent money carefully	**May I help you?** a polite way of asking someone if he or she needs assistance
better days a time in the past when life was easier	**I'll take this.** I'll buy this.
on sale selling at a lower price	**took a seat** sat down

7 Literary Term: Sensory Details

Writers use **sensory details** to create images of the five senses – touch, taste, smell, sight, and sound. For example, to create the image of touching, the author of this story wrote, " . . . her hand was touching something very soft and pleasant." To create the image of tasting, she wrote, "She closed her eyes and remembered the delicious lunch."

Focus As you read the story, notice the sensory details the author uses to create images. Do they help you see, hear, touch, smell, or taste?

About the Author

Kate Chopin (1851–1904) was born Katherine O'Flaherty in St. Louis, Missouri. Her father was born in Ireland, but he had a very successful business in St. Louis. He died when Chopin was very young. Her mother was French Creole,[1] and Chopin was very close to her mother and to her French-speaking grandmother. Chopin had a very interesting life as a child. She spoke both French and English, played the piano, and read many books.

As an adult, Chopin was admired for her independence and intelligence. She married Oscar Chopin, moved to New Orleans, and had six children. However, she wasn't a typical housewife of the late 1800s. When her husband died suddenly, she didn't have any money. She began earning money by writing short stories.

Kate Chopin was one of America's favorite short story writers of her time and is still very popular. Most of her stories deal with women who have difficult lives and who want to be independent.

A Pair of Silk Stockings

Mrs. Sommers was amazed to discover that the money she saved every week was now $15. This was a large amount for someone who watched every penny and was so careful with money. She smiled as she touched her wallet with a feeling of pride.

5   Life was easier years ago. Those were "better days," but now she couldn't think about the past. She was too busy taking care of her family and spending every dollar carefully. Now she had $15 in her wallet!

For several days she walked around thinking about how to spend her treasure. During the quiet hours at night when the children were asleep,
10   she stayed awake making plans to spend the money.

---

[1] **Creole**: in North America, a person who is a mixture of Native American, French, Spanish, European, African, or Caribbean

Perhaps she could spend a dollar more on Janie's shoes, and she could buy Mag a dress. She could buy material to make new shirts for the boys. She could get caps for the boys and hats for the girls. The thought of her four children dressed in new clothes made her excited 15 and happy.

Mrs. Sommers knew the value of bargains. She could stand on line for hours waiting to buy something on sale. She always tried to get the lowest price. But this day she was a little tired. After feeding the children and sending them off to school, she went out on a shopping trip. She 20 was in such a hurry, she forgot to eat lunch.

After entering the department store, Mrs. Sommers stood in front of a counter. She put her hand down on the counter to rest for a few minutes. Suddenly, she realized that her hand was touching something very soft and pleasant. She looked down and saw that her hand was lying on 25 some silk stockings. The sign nearby said the stockings were reduced from $2.50 to $1.98.

A young saleswoman asked, "May I help you choose some silk stockings?"

Mrs. Sommers smiled and stared at the stockings as if they were 30 jewels. She began to blush, "Do you have any stockings in size eight?"

"Oh, yes. What color do you want?" replied the saleswoman. "We have light blue, tan, gray, and black."

"I would like the black, please."

When the saleswoman brought her the stockings, Mrs. Sommers looked at them for a long time. "I'll take this pair," she said. She handed the woman a five-dollar bill and held her hand out waiting for the change and the package. It was such a small package. It seemed to disappear when she dropped it into her old shopping bag.

Then Mrs. Sommers took the elevator to the Ladies Room on the top floor. Here in a corner, she took off her cotton stockings and put on

55 the new silk ones. She was no longer thinking in the practical way she
usually did. She was not thinking at all. The silk felt so wonderful on her
skin. She leaned back in the soft chair and enjoyed the feeling of luxury.
Then she put on her shoes and walked straight to the shoe department.

The clerk spent a lot of time bringing her shoes to try on. Finally, she
60 chose a pair which she wore immediately. Her next stop was the glove
department where she chose a pair
of black leather gloves with small
pearl buttons at the wrists.

Mrs. Sommers felt very happy,
65 and she walked with her head high
and a small smile on her face. She
felt pretty and young again. She also
felt very hungry. Then she noticed
a restaurant she had never been in.
70 She entered and was seated at a table
by herself. She ordered a shrimp
cocktail and a glass of wine. For

> Mrs. Sommers felt very happy, and she walked with her head high and a small smile on her face. She felt pretty and young again.

dessert she had black coffee with a slice of chocolate cake. The restaurant
was very pleasant. Other people were quietly eating and talking. There
75 was soft music playing, and a breeze blew in from the windows. When
she paid her bill, she added a generous tip for the waiter. He bowed as
she left as if she were a princess.

There was still money in her wallet. Her next luxury was going to
see a play. She walked into the theater and sat down just as the play
80 was starting. As the curtain rose, Mrs. Sommers sat back in her seat and
smiled. She laughed at the funny moments and cried at the sad ones.
When the play ended and the music stopped, Mrs. Sommers sat in her
seat a little longer. She was the last one to leave the theater.

Mrs. Sommers waited for the bus on the corner. She climbed onto
85 the bus and took a seat behind the driver. She was no longer smiling.
She began to think about all the things she had to do at home. Then she
remembered her wonderful day. She touched the silk stockings on her
legs. She unbuttoned her soft leather gloves. She closed her eyes and
remembered the delicious lunch. Then she remembered sitting in the
90 theater and watching the play. Deep in her heart there was a powerful
wish. She wished the bus driver would keep driving on and on and never
stop. She wanted this day to last forever.

C UNDERSTANDING THE STORY

1 Reading Comprehension

With a partner or in a small group, discuss the following questions:

1 How does Mrs. Sommers plan to spend the $15 before she goes shopping?
2 What does she actually buy when she goes on her shopping trip?
3 Where does Mrs. Sommers go after she is finished shopping?
4 Why is Mrs. Sommers the last one to leave the theater?
5 Why does she want the bus driver to keep driving forever?

2 Guessing Meaning from Context

The words in the list are in the story. Find the words in the story and try to understand their meanings. Then find the words in the word search box. The words are written across or down. Then use the words to complete the sentences. Use each word only once.

amazed	treasure	generous	blushed
wished	pleasant	bowed	luxury
pride	practical	stared	leaned

```
A  B  D  P  P  R  I  D  E  S  B  Y  D  I  T  C  R  L  S  X  L
Y  L  T  R  E  A  S  U  R  E  L  B  E  S  W  X  C  O  M  Q  E
B  L  U  S  H  E  D  R  N  W  U  A  Q  T  J  C  W  T  D  R  A
O  U  Z  A  M  A  Z  E  D  G  X  P  R  A  C  T  I  C  A  L  N
W  X  T  A  G  E  N  E  R  O  U  S  I  R  Z  A  G  K  O  Y  E
E  U  R  H  W  K  P  I  B  N  R  P  L  E  A  S  A  N  T  Q  D
D  R  W  I  S  H  E  D  X  C  Y  U  V  D  D  L  F  H  W  K  Z
```

1 Mrs. Sommers thought the money she saved was a ____treasure____.

2 She was _____ to find out she had saved $15.

3 She also had a feeling of _____ because she saved so much money.

4 When Mrs. Sommers went to the department store, she _____ on the counter and felt something soft.

5 The stockings felt _____.

6 Mrs. Sommers _____ at the stockings as if they were jewels.

7 Mrs. Sommers _____ when she asked for a pair of stockings.

8 Mrs. Sommers prided herself on being _____ about spending money.

9 Although the silk stockings were a _____, they were on sale.

10 Mrs. Sommers gave the waiter a _____ tip.

11 He _____ to her as if she were a princess.

12 Mrs. Sommers _____ that her day of luxury would last forever.

3 Grammar: Adjectives

Adjectives are words that describe nouns and pronouns. Nouns can also serve as adjectives when they describe other nouns. Without adjectives our writing would be very boring.

● In English, adjectives are usually placed before nouns. An adjective helps us imagine what a place, person, or thing looks like. In the example below, you can see how the adjectives can create a very different picture of a person or a place.

Examples:
A **tall, thin, black-haired** man walked into a **small, dark, ugly** room.
A **short, fat, fair-haired** man walked into a **large, lovely, sunlit** room.

continued

> ● When a sentence has a *be* verb (*is, am, are, was,* or *were*) or a linking verb (*feel, look, smell, taste, sound, become, seem,* etc.), the noun can come before the verb, and the adjective can come after the verb. Think of the linking verb as an equal sign (=).
>
> *Examples:*
> The stockings are **beautiful**.
> The gloves feel **soft**.

Application 1 This story uses many adjectives that help us imagine Mrs. Sommers and the experiences she has in one day. Find the adjectives in the following sentences and underline them. Then circle the nouns they describe.

1 Mrs. Sommers bought a pair of <u>soft</u>, <u>black</u> <u>leather</u> (gloves.)

2 The gloves had small pearl buttons at the wrists.

3 She felt like a pretty young woman again.

4 It was a small package.

5 There was soft music playing.

6 In the theater, she laughed at the funny moments and cried at the sad ones.

7 Then she remembered her wonderful day.

8 Deep in her heart there was a powerful wish.

Application 2 In the following sentences, underline the adjectives and circle the nouns or pronouns they describe.

1 (Mrs. Sommers) is <u>good</u>, <u>caring</u>, and <u>careful</u> with money.

2 The silk felt wonderful on her skin.

3 The gloves felt soft, and they looked beautiful.

4 She felt pretty and young again.

5 She also became very hungry.

6 The coffee and cake tasted delicious.

7 Mrs. Sommers seemed happy buying luxuries for herself.

8 Mrs. Sommers became sad when she rode the bus home.

D THINKING CRITICALLY

1 Discussing the Story

With a partner or in a small group, discuss the following questions:

1 Why does Mrs. Sommers change her plan to buy clothes for her children?
2 Why does Mrs. Sommers blush when she talks to the saleswoman?
3 Do you think it is good that Mrs. Sommers spent all the money on herself? Why or why not?
4 Do you think Mrs. Sommers is sad when she returns home?
5 Have you ever spent a lot of money on yourself? What did you do? How did you feel after you spent the money?

2 Making Inferences

Authors often write something that can have more than one meaning. You need to figure out what the author means. This is called making inferences. Read the following sentences from the story. Then circle the answer that shows the author's meaning. If you need help, look back at the story. Discuss your answers.

1 Mrs. Sommers smiled and stared at the stockings as if they were jewels.
   a Mrs. Sommers really wanted jewelry.
   b She thought the stockings looked very beautiful.
   c The stockings cost as much as jewels.

2 It was such a small package. It seemed to disappear when she dropped it into her old shopping bag.
   a The shopping bag was too big and too old to carry pretty silk stockings.
   b It was easy for Mrs. Sommers to forget that she had bought herself something valuable because the package was so small.
   c It was going to be difficult for Mrs. Sommers to find the package again in her large shopping bag.

3 She felt pretty and young again.
   a She wished she did not have children so she could have more fun.
   b She felt men were looking at her and noticing her.
   c She enjoyed buying new things and taking care of herself.

4 She wanted this day to last forever.
   a Mrs. Sommers didn't want to see her children again.
   b Mrs. Sommers felt bad because the next day she would have no money.
   c Mrs. Sommers didn't want the day to end because she was enjoying herself.

3 Analyzing the Story: Sensory Details

As you read on page 18, authors use sensory details to help you imagine the five senses. The items listed below are from the story. Put them in the correct rows to complete the chart.

1 staring at the stockings
2 listening to the music in the restaurant
3 drinking wine
4 watching the play
5 resting her hand on the counter
6 eating a shrimp cocktail
7 feeling the silk stockings on her legs
8 unbuttoning her leather gloves
9 drinking black coffee
10 feeling the breeze through the open window

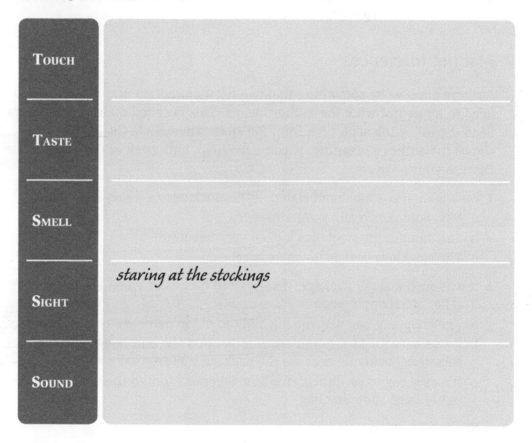

TOUCH	
TASTE	
SMELL	
SIGHT	*staring at the stockings*
SOUND	

Did the author help you imagine Mrs. Sommers's day? Discuss your answer with a partner.

4 Summarizing

Put the following sentences in the correct order to summarize the story. Write the numbers 1 to 6 to show the order. The first one has been done for you.

____ She takes a bus back to her home and is sorry the day is over.

____ She has lunch in a pleasant restaurant.

____ Mrs. Sommers buys a pair of black silk stockings.

____ Mrs. Sommers goes to the theater to see a play.

____ She buys a pair of shoes and some gloves.

_1_ Mrs. Sommers, who is careful about spending money, saves $15.

5 Writing

Pretend you are Mrs. Sommers. Write in your diary about the day you spent in town. Describe what you did. Answer the following questions and try to use sensory details.

Where did you go?

What did you do?

How did you feel?

CHAPTER 3

One Thousand Dollars

O. HENRY

A PREPARING TO READ

1 Think Before You Read

Answer the following questions:

1 What would you do if someone gave you $1,000? Would you spend it, save it, or give it away?
2 Have you ever given money to someone? How did it make you feel?
3 Can money make you happy? Why or why not?

2 Picture Focus

With a partner, talk about the picture. Who are these men? Why do you think one man is giving money to another?

3 Words to Know

Study the following key words from the story. They all relate to *money or property when someone dies*. Then complete the paragraph using each word once.

lawyer someone who gives legal advice	**leave** give something to someone after you die
will a written statement of who should get your money or property when you die	**inherit** receive money or property from someone who has died
deceased a formal way of describing someone who is no longer living; dead	**heirs** people who receive money or property from someone who has died

As you get older, it is important that you write a _____. This statement will say who will _____ your money or property when you are _____. Before you write it, you should go to a _____ to get advice. Normally, people _____ their money or property to their relatives. But your _____ don't have to be your relatives. You can also give your money to your favorite charity or your cat!

4 Story Preview

Read the preview of the story. Then answer the question in Making Predictions on the next page.

Bob Gillian has just received $1,000 from his uncle's will. He has to spend the money and then tell his uncle's lawyers how he spent it. If he can prove that he used the $1,000 wisely and unselfishly, he will get an additional $50,000. Otherwise, another person will inherit the money.

5 Making Predictions

From the Story Preview, try to predict what will happen. Circle one choice below or write your own answer. Discuss your prediction with a partner.

How will Bob Gillian spend the $1,000?

1 He will spend it on a girlfriend.

2 He will lose it.

3 He will give it away.

4 _____

6 Idioms and Expressions

You will find these idioms and expressions in the story:

paid attention to listened carefully to someone or something	**go on stage** appear in a play in a theater
be worth be equal in value to	**Would you mind . . . ?** a polite way to ask for something
depend on need the support of someone or something	**turned white** became scared

7 Literary Term: Character

The people in a story are called **characters**. The most important people in a story are the **main** characters. Other people in the story are **minor** characters. Good writers make you understand the people in their stories. You understand why they do things and how they feel.

Focus As you read this story, decide who the main character is. How do you feel about this character? Does the main character surprise you at the end of the story?

About the Author

O. Henry (1862–1910) was born William Sydney Porter in Greensboro, North Carolina. When he was a young man, he moved to Texas, where he married and worked in a bank.

However, Porter was extremely unlucky in Texas. His young wife was sick, and he was accused of stealing money from the bank. He ran away to Honduras in Central America, but he returned to the United States when he learned that his wife was dying. After her death in 1897, Porter was found guilty and sent to jail for five years. While he was in prison, Porter wrote and sold at least 12 stories and changed his name to O. Henry. When he was released from jail, he moved to New York and wrote for many magazines.

One Thousand Dollars

"What can I do with a thousand dollars?"

"One thousand dollars," repeated Lawyer Tolman, seriously, "and here is the money."

Young Bob Gillian laughed as he picked up the thin package of new
5 fifty-dollar bills. "It's such a difficult amount of money. It's too much to spend and too little to invest," he said. "I'll have to think about it."

Lawyer Tolman said, "You heard the reading of your uncle's will. I do not know if you paid much attention to its details. I want to remind you of one detail. You have to tell us how you spent this $1,000. The will
10 states that clearly. So, I hope you will do as your uncle wished.

"I'll do my best," said the young man politely.

Gillian went to his club. There he looked for his friend Bryson. He found him in a corner reading a book. Gillian interrupted him. "I have a funny story to tell you," he said. "I just came from my deceased uncle's
15 company. He left me one thousand dollars. Now, what can I do with a thousand dollars?"

"I thought," said Bryson, "that your deceased uncle was worth something like half a million."

"He was," answered Gillian, "and that's where the joke comes in. He left his whole fortune to science. The butler and the housekeeper get $10 each. I inherited $1,000."

"Well, you don't have to worry. You've always had plenty of money to spend," said Bryson.

"That's true," Gillian said. "Uncle always gave me money when I asked for it."

"Are there any other heirs?" Bryson asked.

"None," Bob Gillian looked upset. "There is a Miss Hayden, my uncle's secretary, who lived in his house. She's a quiet woman – musical – the daughter of a friend. I forgot to say she got $10 also. But tell me, what can I do with a thousand dollars?"

"You?" said Bryson with a laugh. "You can buy Miss Lotta Lauriere a diamond necklace with the money."

"Thanks," said Gillian, rising. "I thought I could depend on you, Bryson."

Gillian phoned for a cab and said to the driver, "Take me to the stage entrance of the Columbine Theatre."

Miss Lotta Lauriere was putting on makeup in her dressing room when Gillian knocked on the door.

"Come in," said Miss Lauriere. "Oh, it's you, Bobbie. I don't have much time. I go on stage in two minutes."

"It won't take me two minutes, Lotta. How would you like a diamond necklace? I have a thousand dollars."

"Only a thousand?" she asked. "If you can get me the necklace I saw in Tiffany's for three thousand, then I'll be interested."

Gillian opened the door and walked out. He got into a taxi and said to the driver, "Drive until I tell you to stop."

Eight blocks down Broadway, Gillian got out. A blind man on the sidewalk was selling pencils. Gillian stood in front of him and said, "Excuse me, but would you mind telling me what you would do if you had a thousand dollars?"

The blind man answered, "I'm not sure I need a thousand dollars. Here, take a look at this if you like." The blind man took a bank book out of his coat pocket. Gillian opened it. It showed a balance of $1,785 to the blind man's credit.

Gillian returned the book and got into the cab. He told the driver, "Take me to the law offices of Tolman and Sharpe at 1740 Broadway."

When he entered the office, Mr. Tolman looked at him in an unfriendly way. "May I ask you a question?" Gillian said, "Was Miss Hayden left anything in my uncle's will besides $10?"

"Nothing," said the lawyer.

"I thank you very much, Sir," Gillian said, and he went out to his cab. He gave the driver the address of his uncle's home.

Miss Hayden was writing letters. She was small and thin and dressed in black. Gillian greeted her and said, "I've just come from Tolman's office. They've been looking at some papers and found that my uncle left you a thousand dollars. Here it is." Gillian laid the money on the desk.

Miss Hayden turned white. "Oh," she said, and again, "Oh."

Gillian half turned and looked out of the window. "I suppose, of course," he said in a low voice, "that you know I love you."

"I'm sorry," said Miss Hayden, taking the money.

"I guess there is no chance that you feel the same about me?" Gillian asked.

"No, I'm very sorry," she repeated.

"May I write a note?" Gillian asked with a smile. He seated himself at a big table. She gave him paper and a pen, and then quietly went back to her desk.

Gillian wrote how he spent the thousand dollars in these words: "One thousand dollars to the best and dearest woman on earth." He put the note into an envelope and left.

His cab stopped again at the office of Tolman and Sharp.

"I have spent the thousand dollars," Gillian told Mr. Tolman, "and I have come to give you a written report." He laid it on the desk as Tolman opened the door of the safe and called his partner, Sharp.

They took a large envelope out of the safe and Mr. Tolman said, "There is an addition to your uncle's will. It states that if you spent the thousand dollars wisely and unselfishly, you will receive $50,000. If not, Miriam Hayden will get the money."

Tolman reached for the envelope, but Gillian tore it up and said, "You don't need to read this. I'll tell you. I lost the thousand dollars betting on a horse at the race track. Good afternoon, Gentlemen."

Tolman and Sharp shook their heads sadly at each other when Bob Gillian left, for they heard him whistling happily as he waited for the elevator.

C UNDERSTANDING THE STORY

1 Reading Comprehension

With a partner or in a small group, discuss the following questions:

1 What advice does Bryson give Gillian?
2 Why does Lotta Lauriere refuse Gillian's offer to buy her a diamond necklace?
3 Why doesn't Gillian give the $1,000 to the blind man?
4 How does Gillian finally spend the $1,000?
5 Why does Gillian tear up his note to the lawyers?

2 Guessing Meaning from Context

The words in the list are in the story. Read the sentences below from the story. Then circle the letter of the best meaning of the **bold** word in each sentence.

seriously	remind	joke	addition
invest	politely	fortune	unselfishly
details	interrupted	balance	whistling

1 "One thousand dollars," repeated Lawyer Tolman, **seriously**, . . .
   a jokingly
   b without humor
   c in an unfriendly manner

2 "It's too much to spend and too little to **invest**."
   a put in the bank
   b give away
   c buy something to make more money

3 "I do not know if you paid much attention to its **details**."
   a description
   b summaries
   c specific facts and information

4 "I want to **remind** you of one detail."
   a help someone remember
   b help someone review
   c help someone change

5 "I'll do my best," said the young man **politely**.
  a with good manners
  b carelessly
  c without paying attention

6 He found him in a corner reading a book. Gillian **interrupted** him.
  a woke him up
  b stopped him from what he was doing
  c shouted at him

7 ". . . that's where the **joke** comes in."
  a the funny thing
  b mistake
  c trick

8 "He left his whole **fortune** to science."
  a future earnings
  b large amount of money, possessions, or property
  c bank account

9 The blind man took a bank book out of his coat pocket. . . . It showed a **balance** of $1,785 . . .
  a amount of money a person has
  b amount of money owed
  c amount of money spent

10 "There is an **addition** to your uncle's will."
  a change
  b new item
  c mistake

11 "It states that if you spent the money wisely and **unselfishly**, you will receive $50,000."
  a foolishly
  b caring about others
  c intelligently

12 . . . they heard him **whistling** happily as he waited for the elevator.
  a singing
  b making a musical sound with his lips
  c humming

3 Grammar: Adverbs

Adverbs are words that modify (describe, change, or add information to) action verbs, adjectives, and other adverbs. Adverbs also answer the questions of *where, when, how, how much.*

- Adverbs modify verbs. In the following sentence from the story, *seriously* is an adverb because it modifies the verb *repeated.* The adverb here answers the question *how.*

  "One thousand dollars," repeated Lawyer Tolman, **seriously** . . .

- Adverbs modify adjectives. In this sentence from the story, *too* modifies the adjective *little.* The adverb here answers the question *how much.*

  "It's . . . **too** little to invest."

- Adverbs modify other adverbs. In this sentence from the story, *very* modifies the adverb *much.*

  "I thank you **very** much, Sir."

- You will find that many adverbs add *-ly* to the adjective form. However, not all words that end in *-ly* are adverbs. In this sentence from the story, *unfriendly* is an adjective (not an adverb) that modifies *way.*

  Mr. Tolman looked at him in an **unfriendly** way.

- Some adverbs do not have an adjective form. Examples are *just, always, then, again, soon, not, very,* and *never.*

Application 1   In each of the following sentences from the story, there is at least one adverb. Find the adverb and underline it. Then in the space on the right, write the word the adverb modifies.

1 "I'll do my best," said the young man <u>politely.</u>   _____ *said* _____

2 "I just came from my deceased uncle's company."   _____

3 "You've always had plenty of money to spend."   _____

4 She gave him paper and a pen, and then quietly went back to her desk. _____

5 His cab stopped again at the office of Tolman and Sharp. _____

6 "It states that if you spent the thousand dollars wisely and unselfishly, you will receive $50,000." _____

7 Tolman and Sharp shook their heads sadly . . . _____

8 . . . they heard him whistling happily as he waited for the elevator. _____

Application 2   Look at the list of adverbs and adjectives below. Complete the sentences in the paragraph with words from the list. Then put *1* above the adverbs and *2* above the adjectives. Use each word once.

selfishly	bad	careful	carelessly	many
only	politely	serious	very	wisely

The young man listened ____*poli̱tely*____ to his lawyer. His lawyer read

him a will from his uncle. The lawyer was _____

_____ as he read the will. There were _____

details. The young man paid _____ attention to the details. His

uncle was leaving him one thousand dollars. At first, he would get

_____ half of the money. If he spent it _____,

he would get the other half. If he spent it _____ or

_____, he would not get the other half. The young man thought

his uncle's will was a _____ joke.

D THINKING CRITICALLY

1 Discussing the Story

With a partner or in a small group, discuss the following questions:

1 Why doesn't Miss Hayden return Gillian's love?
2 Does Gillian really love Miss Hayden, or does he love Miss Lauriere?
3 What would happen if Gillian did not tear up his note?
4 What do you think Miss Hayden will do with the money?
5 What would you do if you were Gillian?

2 Making Inferences

Authors often write something that can have more than one meaning. You need to figure out what the author means. This is called making inferences. Read the following sentences from the story. Then circle the answer that shows the author's meaning. If you need help, look back at the story. Discuss your answers.

1 ". . . and that's where the joke comes in. He left his whole fortune to science."
   a Gillian thinks his uncle was a funny man.
   b Gillian can't believe his uncle left all his money only to science.
   c Gillian is telling his friend a lie.

2 Gillian said, "Was Miss Hayden left anything in my uncle's will besides $10?"
   a Gillian is thinking of giving his money to Miss Hayden.
   b Gillian wants Miss Hayden's money.
   c Gillian wants to know if Miss Hayden got his uncle's house.

3 "I've just come from Tolman's office. They've been looking at some papers and found that my uncle left you a thousand dollars. Here it is."
   a Gillian wants Miss Hayden to have the one thousand dollars.
   b Gillian is joking with Miss Hayden.
   c Gillian is telling Miss Hayden that the lawyers made a mistake.

4 "I'm sorry," said Miss Hayden, taking the money.

    a She doesn't believe Gillian really loves her.

    b She is being polite.

    c She doesn't love Gillian.

5 Tolman and Sharp shook their heads sadly at each other when Bob Gillian left, for they heard him whistling happily as he waited for the elevator.

    a Tolman and Sharp don't understand why Gillian is happy after losing the $50,000.

    b Tolman and Sharp think Gillian made the right decision.

    c Tolman and Sharp are sad that Gillian's uncle died.

3 Analyzing the Story: Character

As you read on page 30, good writers help you understand the characters in their stories. The chart below has the names of characters in the story. Complete the chart. Add adjectives that describe each character. (Find some adjectives on pages 22–24 in Chapter 2.) Add adverbs to complete the phrases. (Find some adverbs on pages 34, 36, and 37 of this chapter.)

CHARACTERS	ADJECTIVES	ADVERBS
Bob Gillian	*pleasant*	spends money _____
Lawyer Tolman		shook his head _____
Lotta Lauriere	*busy*	speaks ___*quickly*___
Miss Hayden		talks _____
Bryson		listens ___*carefully*___

4 Summarizing

Put the following sentences in the correct order to summarize the story.
Write the numbers 1 to 7 to show the order. The first one has been done
for you.

_____ Gillian writes a note and later tears it up.

_____ Miss Lotta Lauriere refuses Gillian's offer to buy her a
diamond necklace.

_____ Gillian's inheritance will be given to Miss Hayden.

_____ Gillian gives the $1,000 to Miss Hayden.

_1_ In his will, Gillian's uncle gives Gillian $1,000.

_____ Gillian has to tell how he spent the $1,000.

_____ Gillian asks a blind man how he would spend $1,000.

5 Writing

Describe Miss Hayden's life a year after she received the $50,000.

A TAKE A CLOSER LOOK

1 Theme Comparison: Making Choices

Making choices is a theme in all the stories in Part One. Knute Axelbrod decided to go to college later in his life. Mrs. Sommers decided to spend money on herself. Bob Gillian unselfishly decided to give up a $50,000 inheritance.

With a partner, discuss the following questions.

1 Before the three main characters of the stories made their decisions, what were their choices?
2 How did the three characters make their choices? Did anyone help them?
3 Were the three characters happy with their final choices?

2 Freewriting

Write the words *making choices* at the top of a sheet of paper. Then write any words that come into your mind when you think of making choices. For 15 minutes, write about a time in your life when you had to make an important choice. What was the situation? What were your choices? What was your final choice? How did you make your choice?

B REVIEW

1 Grammar Review

Read the following paragraph. Underline all the nouns, circle all the adjectives, and box all the adverbs.

In the (first) story you read, Knute Axelbrod made a [very] (unusual) decision. He decided to go to college, but he was very lonely. He made only one friend, Gil. He and Gil spent one enjoyable evening together. They talked about poetry. In the second story, Mrs. Sommers bought a pair of silk stockings. She also had lunch in an expensive restaurant. Then she saw a wonderful play in the theater. In the final story, Gillian gave away his inheritance to the small quiet secretary of his uncle. He told the two lawyers he spent the money foolishly on a horse race.

2 Vocabulary Review

Discover the vocabulary words by filling in the missing letters. Meanings are given after each word. If you need help, look back at the three stories you read in Part One.

1 a __ d __ __ __ __ __   something added on

2 a __ v __ __ __ __ __ e   an exciting trip or experience

3 a __ __ z __ __   surprised, filled with wonder

4 b __ l __ __ c __   what is left over

5 b l __ __ __   pink color in the face, usually when embarrassed

6 b __ w __ __   bent over to show respect or to say thank you

7 l __ __ n __ __   rested on, such as a hand on a table

8 l __ __ __ l y   feeling sad; being alone

9 l __ x __ __ y   something one doesn't need but wants

10 p __ __ __ s __ __ __   nice

11 p __ l __ __ __ __ y   using good manners

12 p __ __ c __ __ __ __ l   useful

13 p __ __ d __   feeling of worth

14 s __ r __ __ __ s __ y   without humor

15 s __ __ l   spirit, essence of a person

16 s __ __ r __   look at something for a long time

17 s t __ __ __ __   take something that doesn't belong to you

18 s __ r __ __ g __   unusual; odd; unfamiliar

C ELEMENTS OF A SHORT STORY

Filling Out the Elements Chart

This chart shows the five basic elements of a short story. You can find definitions for these elements on page 170. Some of these elements have been filled out for "Young Man Axelbrod." Complete the chart. Then copy the blank chart on page xvi and fill it out for "A Pair of Silk Stockings" or "One Thousand Dollars" or for both stories. Share your charts with a partner or in a small group.

Elements of _____ *Young Man Axelbrod* _____
(name of story)

SETTING

CHARACTERS

PLOT
Knute Axelbrod is a retired farmer who wants to be a scholar. He gets accepted at Yale University. At Yale he becomes lonely and disappointed. Then he meets Gil Washburn. One night they walk in the moonlight and discuss great men and their ideas. Gil reads a book of French poetry and then gives it to Knute. Knute is content, but the next morning he decides to return home.

CONFLICT
The conflict is between Knute's desire to become a serious student and the difficulty he faces because he is no longer young and is different from the other students.

THEME(s)
Sometimes our dreams and plans don't happen the way we want them to. One wonderful experience can make up for many disappointments.

WEBQUEST

Find more information about the topics in Part One by going on the Internet. Go to www.cambridge.org/discoveringfiction/wq and follow the instructions for doing a WebQuest. Have fun. Enjoy the quest!

PART TWO

The Role of Fate

WE OFTEN HEAR a happy couple say on their wedding day, "It was fate that brought us together." Fate, or destiny, is defined as something that happens to us, good or bad, that we cannot change or control. Some people believe this is true. Other people think we are free to make choices and control our own fate. Writers often use the role of fate in literature.

In the first story you are about to read, what seems to be a character's fate changes into a surprise ending. In the second story, the main character is unaware of events that happen to him while he is sleeping. In the final story, two young people fall in love, and the woman's father tries to end their relationship. As you read these stories, ask yourself if any of the characters have control of their own fate.

CHAPTER 4

Omit Flowers

DANA BURNET

A PREPARING TO READ

1 Think Before You Read

Answer the following questions:

1 Why do you think some people stay angry for a long time?
2 Have you ever been very angry at the way a friend treated you? How did you react? What did you do?
3 What are some ways you deal with your anger? How do you become calm again?

2 Picture Focus

With a partner, talk about the picture. Who are the two people? Why do you think the woman is kicking the man out of her house?

3 Words to Know

Study the following key words and expressions from the story. They all relate to *funerals*. Then complete the paragraph using each word once.

funeral a ceremony that takes place after a person dies	**grave** a hole in the ground where the body of a dead person is put
bury put something into the ground and cover with soil	**cemetery** a place where they bury dead people
casket a box that holds the body of a dead person	**mourners** family and friends who go to the funeral; people who are very sad about the death of someone or something
hearse a car or carriage that carries a casket	

A _____ service is held after a person dies. At funerals in the United States, people talk about the person who has died and tell stories about his or her life. The people who attend a funeral to remember the dead person are called _____. The dead person is placed in a _____. This is sometimes called a coffin. The casket is placed in a carriage or car called a _____. The dead person is taken to the _____. Grave-diggers have already dug a _____. Everyone watches as they _____ the person by putting the casket into the ground. The mourners comfort each other on this sad occasion.

4 Story Preview

Read the preview of the story. Then answer the question in Making Predictions on the next page.

Two elderly people have a history of being angry at each other. The old woman, Widow Buxton, thinks she is dying. She calls the old man, who is an undertaker. His job is to make plans for the funeral. Both of them disagree about the cost of the funeral.

5 Making Predictions

From the Story Preview, try to predict what will happen. Circle one choice below or write your own answer. Discuss your prediction with a partner.

What will the two old people do?

1 Widow Buxton will call another undertaker.

2 The undertaker will agree to a cheap funeral.

3 The two old people will become friends.

4 _____

6 Idioms and Expressions

You will find these idioms and expressions in the story:

head of in charge of; the leader	**hale and hearty** healthy and strong
pinching a penny looking for ways to save money	**word got around** a rumor started
put him in his place made the rules of behavior clear	**made up my mind** decided
scrimping and saving not spending very much money and saving it instead	**take it or leave it** accept or reject an offer

7 Literary Term: Local Color

Local color is anything in the story that helps give the reader a clear picture of what the life and times of the story were like. Local color may describe the people's clothing or actions, or the scenery's buildings, landscape, or weather. In this story, local color describes life in a small town and how people know each other's business.

Local color is also revealed through the people's speech. *Regional dialect* is the words, phrases, grammar, and pronunciation that people in a particular region or place use. In this story, we have kept some of the regional dialect of Maine.

Focus As you read the story, notice the dialogue and the way people talk to and about each other. Notice the descriptions of the town, the people, and their possessions.

THE STORY

About the Author

Dana Burnet (1888–1962) was born in Cincinnati, Ohio. He graduated from Cornell University in 1911 with a law degree. Burnet worked as a journalist for the New York *Evening Sun* for seven years. He later worked for *Collier's*, which was a very popular magazine. People liked his writing and looked forward to reading his articles. He also wrote novels and plays. Several plays were produced on Broadway. He moved to Hollywood, California, and wrote scripts for Hollywood movies. He also wrote scripts for television programs.

Omit Flowers

"You busy?" asked a voice from my study doorway.

I turned from my typewriter and saw Willie Lord standing just outside the door. He was in his dress clothes and wore a white shirt with a collar.

"Come in, Willie," I said.

5　　"I been to a funeral," he said, staring at me with his pale, blue eyes. "Was over in Cape Worship, where I was born. Since you're always interested in stories about Maine folks, I thought you might like to hear about it. It was quite a funeral."

"I imagine so. Tell me about it, Willie."

10　　He hesitated, then laughed and started his story.

"I'll have to go back to the beginning and tell you about the Widow[1] Buxton, who I knew when I was a young boy. The Widow was prominent in Cape Worship. She was head of everything a female could be head of including her own family. She had three daughters. Folks said she

15　　married this fellow Buxton after she was jilted by[2] Nehemiah Westfield just to spite Nehemiah. Anyway, Buxton didn't last long.

She was a character. She was the most willful woman that ever lived and the best at pinching a penny. She had her three girls all married at

---

[1]**widow**: a woman whose husband has died, and she has not got married again
[2]**jilted by**: when someone is rejected by the person he or she had agreed to marry

the same time by the same minister to save money. Nehemiah was there
20 because he was an official of the church and was involved in funerals
and weddings. He was a wealthy man and a widower twice. But the
Widow put him in his place.

'Go and sit down, Nehemiah,' she told him. 'You're welcome as a
guest, but I don't expect a bill for any services. I'll manage this wedding
25 myself.'

Nehemiah said it wasn't proper, but she gave him a shove, and he
went into the parlor and sat down.

Well, the three girls had their own homes and gave birth to children.
The Widow was now a grandma, but she went on living in her own
30 house on the Cape and doing her own housework. She was always
scrimping and saving.

The three girls were old married women by now. They were just
waiting for the old Widow to die, but it didn't look as if she ever would.
She was as hale and hearty in her seventies as she was on the day that
35 Nehemiah jilted her at the altar. Then all of a sudden, about two weeks
ago, word got around that she was dying.

Nobody knew what she was dying of. The girls sent for Doc Harmon,
but when he came to her door, she yelled, 'Get out of here. There's
nothing wrong with me. I'm dying, that's all. I made up my mind that
40 it's time for me to go, and nobody's going to stop me.'

Then a week ago, the Widow told the girls to call Nehemiah Westfield.
The girls were surprised because they knew how much she hated him.

Nehemiah came to the house. 'Well, Jenny, (see the Widow's name
was Jenny) this is a sad occasion.'

45 'Don't be a fool. I sent for you because I know you're going to bury
me, and I don't want you to cheat me. What will you charge me for a
good, plain, funeral without any extras?'[3]

'Well, now, Jenny. I can give you the best there is. You can have an
ebony[4] casket with silk lining and solid silver handles. The full service
50 includes the hearse and three carriages. All together it will cost six
hundred and fifty dollars.'

'You want six hundred and fifty dollars! I won't pay such a sinful
price, you old cheat.

I'll give you one hundred dollars to put me in a plain pine[5] coffin and
55 drag me to my grave. If you won't do it for that, I'll send for Jeb Perkins,
the carpenter, and he'll carry me to the cemetery in his truck. He'll do it
cheap just to get rid of me.'

---

[3]**extras:** additional things or items; in this case additional flowers, decorations, and other
items that are part of a funeral
[4]**ebony:** an expensive, hard, black wood used for furniture
[5]**pine:** a cheap, soft wood made from the evergreen tree

Nehemiah was about ready to cry. 'A hundred dollars, Jenny. I've been waiting all these years to bury you nice and comfortable!'

'Nice and profitable, you mean. A hundred dollars, take it or leave it,' she says.

'All right, all right, Jenny. But there's one thing. You've got to have the extras. You've got to have plenty of flowers. You need roses and lilies to cover the casket. Otherwise, if folks see how cheap it is, I'll be ruined.'

'I don't need flowers. That's foolishness. If you want flowers, there's a hydrangea bush[6] behind my house. If you want to cover the coffin, you can cover it with hydrangeas.'

'I won't do it,' says Nehemiah.

'Then get out of my house. I'm sick of the sight of you anyway, Nehemiah Westfield.'

'And I'm sick of you. You're a penny pinching, bad-tempered, willful old woman and I thank the good Lord I never married you.'

Well, sir, when he said that, the Widow rose up out of bed like a cow moose[7] coming out of a snowdrift. Her whole family was standing around the bed. She landed on her feet and let out one long screech. Then she lunged for Nehemiah.

Nehemiah didn't stop to think that she was a dying woman. He yelled and ran for the door. The Widow ran after him. Just as he got to the front door and opened it, she caught up to him.

'You skinny old gravedigger,' she yelled. 'I wouldn't have married you if you were the last man on earth.' Then she kicked him from behind, and he went flying out the door.

Nehemiah's feet never touched the front steps. He sailed right out onto the lawn, came down on his feet and kept on running. The Widow stood on the doorstep watching him and laughing. She was still laughing when all her children and soon-to-be mourners came down the stairs and surrounded her. They brought her into the parlor and sat her in a chair. She just kept laughing till the girls called Doc Harmon. He came by and gave her medicine to quiet her."

"Well," I joked, "did the Widow stay quiet for her funeral?"

Willie looked at me and said, "It wasn't the Widow Buxton's funeral I went to this morning. It was Nehemiah Westfield's funeral. It seems after the Widow kicked him out, he went home and died of shock. But it was quite a funeral."

"And what happened to the Widow?"

"She was there sitting in the front pew admiring the flowers and looking like she'll live another hundred years."

Willie scratched his head and grinned toothlessly.

"The Widow sent hydrangeas."

---

[6]**hydrangea bush**: a multicolored bush of flowers in small clusters or bunches

[7]**cow moose**: a large animal in the deer family

C UNDERSTANDING THE STORY

1 Reading Comprehension

With a partner or in a small group, discuss the following questions:

1 Where does the story take place? Who are the main characters?
2 Why does Widow Buxton ask Nehemiah to visit her at her home?
3 Why does Widow Buxton kick Nehemiah out of her house?
4 Who dies at the end of the story? What is the cause of death?

2 Guessing Meaning from Context

The words in the list are in the story. Find the words in the story, and try to understand their meanings. Then answer the questions that follow the list. Use your own opinions, knowledge, or experiences.

folks	hesitated	prominent	spite
willful	minister	shove	occasion
fool	cheat	comfortable	pew

1 Why is a **willful** person difficult to have as a friend?

A willful person always wants to have his or her own way.

2 What job does a **minister** do?

_____

3 Describe a time someone tried to **cheat** you.

_____

4 What is another word for **folks**?

_____

5 Why do we say a funeral is a sad **occasion**?

_____

6 Why do you think Willie **hesitated** before starting the story?

_____

7 Give an example of a **prominent** person.

_____

8 What does it mean to **shove** someone?

_____

9 When was the last time you called someone a **fool**?

_____

10 What might someone do to **spite** another person who has hurt their feelings?

_____

11 How do you make people feel **comfortable** when they come to your house?

_____

12 Where would you find a long wooden **pew**?

_____

3 Grammar: Count and Noncount Nouns

Common nouns are either count or noncount.

● Count nouns can be counted (you can use *one*, *two*, *three*, etc., with count nouns). Count nouns can be singular or plural.

Example:
She had three **daughters**.

continued

To make a plural of most count nouns, add *-s, -es,* or *-ies* to the singular noun.

Examples of regular plural forms:

SINGULAR	PLURAL
door	doors
church	churches
family	families
story	stories
cemetery	cemeteries

To make the plural of irregular count nouns, learn the irregular forms.

Examples of irregular plural forms:

SINGULAR	PLURAL
man	men
woman	women
wife	wives
child	children
person	people

- Noncount nouns cannot be counted in English (unless you add words such as *a piece of, a glass of, a cup of* + a noncount noun).

Examples of noncount nouns:
laughter, anger, sugar, water, sand

Noncount nouns are always singular. When they are used as subjects, they are followed by a singular verb.

Examples of noncount nouns as subjects:
<u>Laughter</u> *is* good medicine.
The <u>anger</u> she feels for Nehemiah *goes* back many years.
<u>Sand</u> in the ocean *is* not measurable.

Be careful. Don't add *-s* to these common noncount nouns:
homework, information, equipment, money, luggage

Application 1 Look at the following sentences. In the chart next to the sentences, check ✓ count noun or noncount noun for each word in bold. Then write the plural form of the count nouns. Use a dictionary or the grammar charts on this page to help you.

	Count Noun	Noncount Noun	Plural Form
1 Willie Lord had a **story** to tell.	✓	___	*stories*
2 There was much **interest** in his story.	___	___	_____
3 Widow Buxton was the head of her **family**.	___	___	_____
4 All three girls were married in a **church**.	___	___	_____
5 The Widow did her own **housework**.	___	___	_____
6 She kicked him out the **door**.	___	___	_____
7 All her **children** came down the stairs.	___	___	_____
8 It was Nehemiah Westfield's **funeral**.	___	___	_____
9 Widow Buxton was sitting in the front **pew**.	___	___	_____

Application 2 Look at the following paragraphs. Underline all the common nouns. Then above each common noun write *CS* for singular count noun or *CP* for plural count noun. Put *NC* above all noncount nouns. Use a dictionary to help you.

Widow Buxton was an angry woman. When she was young, Nehemiah Westfield left her on her wedding day. She married another man and had three children. After her husband died, Widow Buxton was very careful with money and didn't spend very much.

When she became older, she lived alone in her own house. She didn't seem to care what people thought about her. One day she called her daughters and told them she was going to die. They called the doctor, and they called the undertaker, Nehemiah. Widow Buxton wanted a simple funeral. Nehemiah wanted her to spend a lot of money. They could not agree, and an argument started.

Widow Buxton kicked Nehemiah out of her house, and her anger turned into laughter.

In the end, Widow Buxton didn't die but went to Nehemiah's funeral instead.

D THINKING CRITICALLY

1 Discussing the Story

With a partner or in a small group, discuss the following questions:

1 Why do you think Nehemiah Westfield chose not to marry Jenny Buxton?
2 What kind of person do you think Widow Buxton is? Which sentences in the story tell you this?
3 How do Widow Buxton's daughters feel about her? Why do you think they feel this way?
4 What parts of the story are funny? Why are they funny?
5 Why does the author choose Willie to tell the story?

2 Making Inferences

Authors often write something that can have more than one meaning. You need to figure out what the author means. This is called making inferences. Read the following sentences from the story. Then circle the answer that shows the author's meaning. If you need help, look back at the story. Discuss your answers.

1 He was in his dress clothes and wore a white shirt with a collar.
   a Willie Lord was a very important person.
   b Willie Lord was dressed for a special occasion.
   c Willie Lord was coming from a soccer game.

2 Anyway, Buxton didn't last long.
   a Mr. Buxton died.
   b Mr. Buxton ran away.
   c Mr. Buxton divorced Jenny.

3 I've been waiting all these years to bury you nice and comfortable.
   a Nehemiah wants Jenny to have a big funeral because he loves her.
   b Nehemiah wants to look good at Jenny's funeral.
   c Nehemiah thinks Jenny is very rich.

3 Analyzing the Story: Local Color

As you read on page 48, local color gives the reader a clear idea of the time and place of the story. Complete the chart with line numbers from the story that match the descriptions of local color in the right-hand column of the chart.

LINES	WHAT THE LINES TELL YOU
Lines _11_ to _14_	Cape Worship is a small town where people know other people's business and talk about it freely.
Lines ___ to ___	People say what is on their mind and speak plainly.
Lines ___ to ___	In Cape Worship, a person's local reputation is everything.
Lines ___ to ___	Cape Worship is a very rural town and the climate is cold.

4 Summarizing

Put the following sentences in the correct order to summarize the story. Write the numbers 1 to 7 to show the order. The first one has been done for you.

____ Nehemiah runs away from Widow Buxton's house.

_1_ Widow Buxton is jilted by Nehemiah Westfield.

____ The daughters send for Doc Harmon.

____ Nehemiah attends the daughters' wedding.

____ Jenny tells her daughters she's dying.

____ Widow Buxton asks Nehemiah to plan a simple funeral.

____ Widow Buxton attends Nehemiah's funeral.

5 Writing

Imagine you are a newspaper reporter for the *Cape Worship News*. Interview Widow Buxton, and ask her to tell you about Nehemiah Westfield. Write your questions and then have a partner answer them as the Widow would. Then change roles and answer your partner's questions.

Two questions you could start with are: *How long did you know Nehemiah Westfield? Was he a good friend of yours?*

CHAPTER 5

David Swan

NATHANIEL HAWTHORNE

A PREPARING TO READ

1 Think Before You Read

Answer the following questions:

1 Look at the definition of fate at the beginning of Part Two. Do you believe fate controls your future, or do you believe you control your future?
2 Have you ever been lucky and missed something bad that could have happened to you? What happened?
3 Do you want to know what is going to happen to you tomorrow? Next year? In 20 years? Why or why not?

2 Picture Focus

With a partner, talk about the picture. Why are people looking at the sleeping young man?

3 Words to Know

Study the following key words and expressions from the story. They all relate to *sleep*. Then complete the paragraph using each word or expression once.

sleepy so tired that you feel you want to go to sleep **pillow** a soft object you put your head on when you are resting or sleeping **fall asleep** start to sleep	**take a nap** go to sleep for a short time, usually in the daytime **sleep soundly** sleep well **awaken** make someone stop sleeping **wake up** stop sleeping

Some people don't _____ _____ at night even

in a comfortable bed with a nice soft _____ under their head.

A small noise can _____ them. So when they

_____ _____ the next day, they are still tired.

To get more sleep, these people sometimes _____

_____ _____ during the day. And because they

do that, it is even more difficult for them to _____

_____ the next night. They just don't feel _____.

4 Story Preview

Read the preview of the story. Then answer the question in Making Predictions on the next page.

David Swan is a young man from New Hampshire. He is going to Boston to work as a clerk in his uncle's grocery store. While he is waiting for the stagecoach* that will take him to Boston, he falls asleep. While he is sleeping, three events happen. Each event could change his life forever.

* **stagecoach**: an old form of public transportation; a large, wheeled carriage pulled by horses

5 Making Predictions

From the Story Preview, try to predict what will happen. Circle one choice below or write your own answer. Discuss your prediction with a partner.

What will happen to David while he is sleeping?

1 David will miss the coach and lose his new job.

2 A pretty girl will stop and look at David.

3 Someone will rob David while he is sleeping.

4 _____

6 Idioms and Expressions

You will find these idioms and expressions in the story:

on foot walking **a shady spot** a place that is not directly in the sun **have in mind** think of a plan or idea **out of sight** so you cannot be seen	**make a living** work for the money that pays your living expenses **I'll bet you.** People say this when they are sure that something is true.

7 Literary Term: Plot

The **plot** of a story is the events that happen from the beginning of the story to the end.

Focus As you read the story, notice all the events that happen. Notice how many of these events David, the main character, is unaware of.

About the Author

Nathaniel Hawthorne (1804–1864) was born in Salem, Massachusetts. His father was the captain of a sailing ship and died when Hawthorne was only four years old. Hawthorne went to live with his mother's large family. As a young man he read a lot. By the time he was 16, he had read almost all of Shakespeare's plays.

In 1821, Hawthorne entered Bowdoin College in Maine. There he met Henry Wadsworth Longfellow, a famous American author, and Franklin Pierce, the future president of the United States. After his graduation, Hawthorne spent the next 12 years writing. His first published book was *Twice Told Tales*, a collection of stories. "David Swan" is one of the stories. Later, Hawthorne wrote his most famous book, *The Scarlet Letter*.

When Franklin Pierce became president, he appointed Hawthorne the United States Consul at Liverpool, England. Hawthorne lived in England and Italy for many years. In 1864, he died suddenly on a trip with President Pierce.

David Swan

David Swan, a young man of 20, was traveling on foot from New Hampshire to Boston. He was going to Boston to work as a clerk in his uncle's grocery store. It was a very hot day, and after walking all morning in the sun, he became tired and sleepy. He found a shady spot
5   where he could sit and wait for a stagecoach. He made a pillow with the small bag of clothes he was carrying, and he put the pillow under his head. Soon David fell asleep.

While David took his nap in the shade, other people passed by him. They were walking, riding horses, or sitting in carriages. Some people
10   didn't notice David. Others laughed to see how soundly he slept. One middle-aged woman looked at him and thought he looked charming in his sleep. Another rather serious-looking man thought David looked

drunk. As David slept, he was completely unaware of these people and what they were thinking.

15   After a few minutes, a brown carriage, pulled by a pair of large horses, stopped in front of the sleeping young man. A wheel of the carriage was broken and had to be fixed. A wealthy old man and his wife stepped out of the carriage and noticed David. The woman said to her husband, "What a beautiful young man! Doesn't he look like our dead son, Henry?
20   Shall we awaken him?"

"Why?" her husband asked, "We know nothing of his character. What do you have in mind?"

"Perhaps fate sent him to us." she replied. "Since the death of our only child, we have no one to give our money to when we die."

25   "Do you think he is as innocent as he looks?" her husband asked.

"Yes, let's awaken him."

But just then the driver called out, "The wheel is fixed. The carriage is ready to leave."

The old couple hurried into the carriage. They felt foolish for thinking
30   they should awaken the stranger.

Meanwhile, David Swan enjoyed his nap.

Soon a pretty young girl walked along and stopped to fix her skirt.

She blushed when she saw David asleep in the shade. Suddenly, a large bee landed on David's face. Without thinking, the young girl pushed the bee away with her handkerchief.

"How handsome he is!" the young girl thought as she looked at David sleeping.

Now, this girl's father was a rich man, and he was looking for a young man like David to work for him and marry his daughter. But the girl was too shy to wake David, so she walked away. Here again, David was unaware that good fortune was close to him.

After the girl was out of sight, two evil-looking men came to the spot where David slept. These men made their living by stealing from other people. Finding David asleep, one man said to the other, "Do you see that bag under his head?"

The second man nodded.

The first man said, "I'll bet you he has money in that bag. Let's take it."

"But what if he wakes up?" the second man asked.

The first man opened his coat and showed his friend a large knife.

The two men approached the sleeping David. One man held his knife near David while the other man looked in David's bag.

At that moment, a dog came between the two men.

"We can't do anything now. The dog's master must be near." The two men ran from the spot while David continued to sleep. This time, David was unaware that death was close to him.

> After the girl was out of sight, two evil-looking men came to the spot where David slept.

A few minutes later, a stagecoach came. David quickly woke up when he heard the noisy wheels of the coach.

"Hello, driver," David shouted, "Will you take another passenger?"

"Sure!" answered the driver.

David climbed up to the seat next to the driver, and the stagecoach continued along the road to Boston.

That afternoon, while David slept, he was unaware of three events that could have changed his destiny. In that one hour, David Swan never knew that fate almost brought him wealth, love, and death.

C UNDERSTANDING THE STORY

1 Reading Comprehension

With a partner or in a small group, discuss the following questions:

1 Why is David traveling from New Hampshire to Boston?
2 What does the wealthy old woman want to give David?
3 What could the pretty young girl's father give David?
4 What do the evil-looking men want from David?

2 Guessing Meaning from Context

The words in the list are in the story. Read the sentences below from the story. Then circle the letter of the best meaning of the bold word in each sentence.

carriages	unaware	foolish	nodded
charming	character	handsome	approached
drunk	innocent	evil	passenger

1 They were walking, riding horses, or sitting in **carriages**.
   a cars
   b coaches pulled by horses
   c park benches

2 One middle-aged woman looked at him and thought he looked **charming** in his sleep.
   a like a nice man
   b like a poor man
   c like a baby

3 Another rather serious-looking man thought David looked **drunk**.
   a very dark and dangerous
   b like he had had too much alcohol
   c sick

4 As David slept, he was completely **unaware** of these people and what they were thinking.
   a not knowing
   b not interested
   c not showing

5 "Do you think he is as **innocent** as he looks?" her husband asked.

   a young

   b healthy

   c good and kind

6 "Why?" her husband asked, "We know nothing of his **character**."

   a life

   b education

   c qualities

7 The old couple hurried into the carriage. They felt **foolish** for thinking they should awaken the stranger.

   a happy

   b unwise

   c sad

8 "How **handsome** he is!" the young girl thought as she looked at David sleeping.

   a rich

   b attractive

   c unintelligent

9 After the girl was out of sight, two **evil**-looking men came to the spot where David slept.

   a angry

   b strange

   c bad

10 The second man **nodded**.

   a moved his head to agree

   b moved his head to disagree

   c said nothing

11 The two men **approached** the sleeping David.

   a came close to

   b hit

   c looked carefully at

12 "Hello, driver," David shouted. "Will you take another **passenger**?"

   a bag

   b direction

   c person

3 Grammar: Articles

A, an, and *the* are called articles. Articles come before nouns. There are many rules for using articles. The following are some basic ones.

- Articles with singular count nouns Use *a* or *an* with singular count nouns when you are giving new or general information to your listener or reader. Use *the* with singular count nouns when you are giving the information for the second time or when the information is specific.

  Be careful. Use *an* instead of *a* before a vowel sound.

  Examples:
  David made **a** pillow. He put **the** pillow under his head.
  He slept for **an** hour. Many things happened to David during **the** hour.
  (Hour does not begin with a vowel letter, but it begins with a
      vowel sound.)

- Articles with plural count nouns Do not use any article for plural count nouns when you are giving new or general information to your listener or reader. Use *the* for plural count nouns when you are giving information for the second time or when the information is specific.

  Examples:
  They were riding horses or sitting in carriages.
  The horses were large, and **the** carriages were beautiful.

- Articles with noncount nouns Do not use *a* or *an* for noncount nouns.

  Do not use any article when the noncount noun is giving general information.

  Use *the* for noncount nouns when they are specific.

  Examples:
  I like money.
  Thank you for **the** money you lent me.

Application 1   In the following sentences, fill in the blank lines with *a*, *an*, or *the*. If no article is necessary, leave the line blank.

1 __A__ carriage stopped in front of David. A wealthy old couple was sitting in __the__ carriage.

2 _____ girl saw David sleeping. _____ girl thought that David was handsome.

3 The girl saw _____ bee on David's face. She pushed _____ bee away.

4 _____ evil-looking man saw David sleeping. _____ man wanted to take David's bag.

5 Soon _____ dog came. The men ran away when they saw _____ dog.

6 A stagecoach, filled with _____ passengers, came. _____ passengers were on their way to Boston.

7 David looked for _____ seat. He took _____ seat next to the driver.

Application 2   Circle the correct noun phrase for each sentence.

1 David, *a young man of 20* / *young man of 20* / *a young men of 20*, was traveling to Boston.

2 The carriage was pulled by a pair of *the horses* / *horses* / *horse*.

3 *A middle-aged widow* / *An middle-aged widow* / *Middle-aged widow* looked at David.

4 A wealthy old man and his wife looked at David. *Old woman* / *An old woman* / *The old woman* said to her husband, "What a beautiful young man!"

5 A girl pushed a bee away from David's face with *handkerchief* / *handkerchiefs* / *a handkerchief*.

6 Two men tried to steal *a bags* / *a bag* / *bag* from David.

7 David lost his chance for *a wealth and happiness* / *wealth and happiness* / *the wealth and happiness*.

D THINKING CRITICALLY

1 Discussing the Story

With a partner or in a small group, discuss the following questions:

1 What do you think might happen if the pretty young girl awakens David?
2 Why does the wealthy old woman think fate sent David to her and her husband?
3 Do you think David is more a lucky man or an unlucky man? Explain your answer.
4 Do you think David will work hard in his uncle's store when he gets to Boston? Why or why not?
5 What does the story tell us about fate?

2 Making Inferences

Authors often write something that can have more than one meaning. You need to figure out what the author means. This is called making inferences. Read the following sentences from the story. Then circle the answer that shows the author's meaning. If you need help, look back at the story. Discuss your answers.

1 The old couple hurried into the carriage. They felt foolish for thinking they should awaken the stranger.
   a The couple was sorry that they missed their chance to meet David.
   b The couple realized it was a bad idea to awaken David.
   c The couple was afraid of David and wanted to get away quickly.

2 She blushed when she saw David asleep in the shade.
   a The girl thought that David was very attractive and that she might fall in love with him.
   b The girl was thinking that her father would be pleased that she found a possible husband.
   c The girl's face got red because she was feeling hot on such a hot and sunny day.

3 "But what if he wakes up?" the second man asked. The first man opened his coat and showed his friend a large knife.
   a The first man was going to kill David if he woke up.
   b The first man wanted to kill his friend.
   c The first man wanted his friend to see how brave he was.

3 Analyzing the Story: Plot

As you read on page 60, the plot is the events that happen in a story. A good way to remember the plot is to make a time line and show the events in the order they happened. The plot of "David Swan" has several events that happen while David is sleeping. Put the events in the time line. Use your own words. Work with a partner.

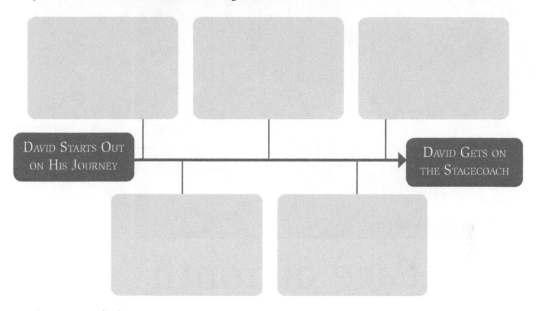

4 Summarizing

Put the following sentences in the correct order to summarize the story. Write the numbers 1 to 7 to show the order. The first one has been done for you.

____ A pretty girl pushes away a bee that is on David's face.

____ A dog saves David from being killed.

____ While waiting for the stagecoach, David falls asleep.

____ Two evil men try to take David's bag.

____ An elderly couple almost decides to awaken David and adopt him.

____ A middle-aged woman stares at David and admires his face.

_1_ David Swan is on his way to Boston to work in his uncle's store.

5 Writing

Describe what you think David's life is like when he lives in Boston.

CHAPTER 6

The Pace of Youth

STEPHEN CRANE

A PREPARING TO READ

1 Think Before You Read

Answer the following questions:

1 How do you know when you are in love with someone? What happens to you?
2 Did you ever have a boyfriend or girlfriend your parents didn't like? What did your parents say or do when they didn't like the boyfriend or girlfriend?
3 Should parents let their children love anyone the children want? Why or why not?

2 Picture Focus

With a partner, talk about the picture. Who is the man looking out the window? Why does he look angry?

3 Words to Know

Study the following key words and expressions from the story. They all relate to *people having feelings for each other*. Then complete the paragraph using each word or expression once.

make eyes at stare at someone and try to get his or her attention because you like that person **smile** when the corners of your mouth are turned up to show you are happy	**fall in love** begin to love another person **hold hands** have one hand holding another person's hand **passion** strong, deep feeling of love, hatred, or anger

When two people _____ _____ _____,
they show their feelings for each other in different ways. At a party, they
might _____ _____ _____ each other
and not pay attention to other people around them. You can see a
_____ on their faces as they talk with each other. They usually
_____ _____ as they walk together. Because they are
young, they think their _____ will last forever.

4 Story Preview

Read the preview of the story. Then answer the question in Making Predictions on the next page.

> This is a story about two young people, Frank and Lizzie, who fall in love. They both work for the young woman's father, Stimson, who owns a merry-go-round. The young man and woman often smile and stare at each other while they are working. The father does not like their relationship and warns them to stop looking at each other.

5 Making Predictions

From the Story Preview, try to predict what will happen. Circle one choice below or write your own answer. Discuss your prediction with a partner.

What will happen to the young couple?

1 The young man will find a new girlfriend.

2 The young woman will obey her father and stop paying attention to the young man.

3 The young couple will get married.

4 _____

6 Idioms and Expressions

You will find these idioms and expressions in the story:

show off do something to attract attention to yourself	**catch up** reach someone or something that is ahead of you
business as usual everything is normal	**run away together** leave family and friends far away so that you can live together or get married
come to the rescue help someone who is in trouble	**take off** leave quickly

7 Literary Term: Theme

A story's **theme** is the author's main idea or purpose in writing the story. It is what the author wants us to think about when we have finished reading. A good author doesn't tell readers directly what the theme of the story is. Readers have to find the theme as they read. The characters, setting, and plot create the theme. Sometimes a story has several themes.

Focus As you read the story, think about the theme and what opinion the author is trying to share with you.

About the Author

Stephen Crane (1871–1900) is most famous for his novel *The Red Badge of Courage*, which was published in 1895. *The Red Badge of Courage* is the story of a soldier in the American Civil War. It is one of the first modern novels about war.

Crane, the son of a Methodist minister, was born in Newark, New Jersey. He briefly attended college and then moved to New York City to become a writer and journalist.

Crane spent his last two years living in England and died in Germany at age 28. Some of his other famous works are *The Open Boat* and *Maggie: A Girl of the Streets*. "The Pace of Youth" takes place in the 1890s and is one of Crane's lighter stories. It deals with love and youth instead of war and death.

The Pace of Youth

S timson stood in the corner of his office staring at the young man. "He must stop making eyes at Lizzie. If he doesn't stop, I'll take away his job."

Then Stimson looked up at the sign, "Stimson's Mammoth Merry-
5 Go-Round." The sign was huge. Each letter was six feet tall. It glowed with light and could be seen from three blocks away. He stood proudly looking at the sign. He heard the sound of the ocean mixed with the voices of people on the beach. As he looked to the north, he saw the horizon where the sky met the sea. He saw a sailboat far out in the water
10 and a bird drifting slowly in the air.

Stimson then looked back at his merry-go-round. There was a circle of animals – lions, giraffes, camels, and horses. They were painted in bright colors and shined in the mirrors in the center of the merry-go-round. Their wooden legs moved up and down in an endless race while
15 the music played.

Stimson could hear children laughing as they sat on the colorful animals and pretended to be in a real race. Some parents rode with the

very young children who couldn't ride alone. A young man stood on top of the narrow wooden platform making sure the children did not get hurt
20 on the merry-go-round.

This young man was the one Stimson was angry at. His name was Frank, and he and Lizzie looked at each other many times during the day. Lizzie worked in a ticket booth near the merry-go-round. Frank looked at Lizzie, and Lizzie looked at Frank.

25 Sometimes Lizzie saw Frank staring at her. She would then turn her head quickly to show that she wasn't interested in him. At other times, she worried about him falling off the narrow wooden platform. Frank showed off by standing very close to its edge. The relationship between these two young people continued in silence. They communicated with
30 smiles and stares.

One day, Stimson walked over to Frank and said, "This must stop."

Frank couldn't understand how Stimson knew about his love for Lizzie. Stimson continued, "I see you making eyes at my daughter, and I see her smiling at you. If you want to keep your job, stop this nonsense."

35 Frank was quiet as Stimson turned around and walked to the ticket booth. Stimson approached Lizzie and said, "Stop smiling at that fool. I told him, and I'm telling you. Stop staring and smiling. You have work to do."

Lizzie was very quiet, too. She didn't look at her father and just
40 played with the money on the shelf in the ticket booth. Stimson walked away smiling. He was proud of his behavior.

"That's the end of that. There'll be no more nonsense around here. It will be business as usual."

Then he stood outside smoking a cigar and watching his merry-go-
45 round.

One evening, a week later, Lizzie's friend Jennie came over to the ticket booth and asked Lizzie if she wanted to walk along the beach after work. Frank saw them talking and followed them. At first, Frank was afraid to approach the girls because he remembered Stimson's warning.
50 He was a coward, but then he found the courage to get closer. In a weak voice he called out, "Lizzie."

Lizzie turned suddenly and said, "Frank, you scared me."

"I'm sorry," Frank said.

Then Jennie came to the rescue. "Come and walk on the beach with
55 us, Frank."

Frank smiled and joined them. After a while, Jennie said, "I'd like to sit here and look at the sea. You two go on. I'll catch up with you later."

They asked her to join them, but she said no. Finally, the young couple walked on without her.

60 "Jennie's really nice," said Lizzie.

"Yes, she is," Frank agreed.

They walked silently. Then Lizzie said, "You were angry at me last week."

"No, I wasn't."

65 "Yes, you were. You didn't look at me once."

"No, I wasn't angry. I was just pretending."

"Oh, were you?" Lizzie said laughing.

Frank looked at Lizzie and knew he was falling in love with her. They held hands and walked back along the beach. When they came back to
70 where Jennie was sitting, she could see the love in their eyes and in their smiles.

A few weeks later, Stimson had to go to the city. When he returned, he found the man who sold popcorn sitting in the ticket booth. Nobody was standing on the wooden platform.

75 "Where is Lizzie?" he asked the popcorn man.

"They went to your house."

Stimson ran to his house and found his wife crying.

"Where's Lizzie?" he yelled.

"Oh, John. They ran away together. They drove by in the horse and
80 carriage a few minutes ago so Lizzie could say goodbye. Before I could ask where they were going, they took off."

"Get my rifle.[1] Do you hear? Get my rifle."

Stimson always told his wife what to do, and she always obeyed. But this time she said, "No, John, not the rifle."

85 Stimson ran down the street looking for a horse and carriage. He found one and jumped in the back. He told the driver to follow Frank and Lizzie's carriage. The driver pushed the horse as hard as he could, and Stimson stood up like a general riding into battle.

90 "Hurry, hurry. Make your horse go faster, faster."

The carriage ahead of them went faster, and soon the distance between them grew larger and larger. The young couple with the energy
95 of youth flew ahead. They had the power of dreams. They flew with the pace of youth. They would fly into the future with hope and passion.

At last, the driver said to Stimson, "It's no good. We can't catch them."

100 Stimson knew he had lost. He was just a powerless old man. He was hot and tired and his head felt cool. He touched his head and realized he forgot his hat.

---

[1]**rifle**: a long gun

C UNDERSTANDING THE STORY

1 Reading Comprehension

With a partner or in a small group, discuss the following questions:

1 How do Frank and Lizzie communicate with each other while they are working?
2 What kind of man is Mr. Stimson? Describe him.
3 How do Frank and Lizzie behave around Mr. Stimson?
4 How does Mrs. Stimson behave around her husband?
5 How does Jennie help Frank and Lizzie?

2 Guessing Meaning from Context

Application 1 The words on the left are in the story. Find the words in the story, and try to understand their meanings. Then match each word to the correct definition on the right. Write the letter of the definition on the blank line.

_e_ 1 pretend   **a** the way a person does or says things

___ 2 narrow   **b** really mad at someone or about something

___ 3 communicate   **c** how fast or slow someone walks or runs

___ 4 nonsense   **d** the ability to be active without becoming tired

___ 5 behavior   **e** act as if something is true when it is not

___ 6 warning   **f** the length of space between two places

___ 7 coward   **g** ability to do dangerous or difficult things

___ 8 courage   **h** not wide; a small distance from one side to the other

___ 9 couple

___ 10 angry   **i** do what someone tells you to do

___ 11 obey   **j** someone who is not brave

___ 12 distance   **k** two people or things together

___ 13 energy   **l** talk or write to someone; send a message through one's behavior

___ 14 pace   **m** foolish words or actions

     n something that tells or shows you that something bad will happen

Application 2 Find the words from Application 1 in the word search box. The words are written across or down.

```
A N G R Y Z C O U R A G E L Q E P I O E U
S A R N O N S E N S E P G J W A R N I N G
D R A C O M M U N I C A T E K Q E B M E F
K R W G B D I S T A N C E H R B T A W R J
I O M B E H A V I O R E I A D T E Q C G V
E W Q S Y Z R C O W A R D X W O N P I Y B
C O U P L E A W L Q F V S P Y X D N R E X
```

3 Grammar: Pronouns

Pronouns are words that can replace nouns. There are different types of pronouns. Two basic types are *subject* pronouns and *object* pronouns.

● Subject pronouns are *I, you, he, she, it, we,* and *they*. They are used as the subjects of verbs.

Example:
Stimson was angry. **He** did not want Frank and Lizzie looking at each other.

● Object pronouns are *me, you, him, her, it, us,* and *them*. They are used as the objects of verbs or of prepositions.

Examples:
Jennie and Lizzie walked down the beach. Frank followed **them**. (object of the verb *followed*)
Frank and Lizzie were in love. Jennie could see the love between **them**. (object of the preposition *between*)

● When you use a pronoun, it must be the same gender (masculine or feminine) or number (singular or plural) as the noun it replaces.

Examples:
Frank = he / him
Lizzie = she / her
Frank and Lizzie = they / them
the merry-go-round = it

Application 1   The following paragraph has eight subject pronouns and nine object pronouns. Circle the subject pronouns and underline the object pronouns.

Frank and Lizzie worked for Stimson's Mammoth Merry-Go-Round. During the day, (they) made eyes at each other. Sometimes Lizzie saw Frank staring at her. She would pretend she wasn't interested in him. Frank didn't know that Lizzie was in love with him, but Frank was in love with her. Stimson did not want Frank and Lizzie to look at each other. He told them to stop it. Later they ran away. Stimson's wife told him that they left in a carriage. Stimson could see it in the distance, and he realized he could not catch up with them.

Application 2   The following sentences are from the story. Circle the subject or object pronouns in b, and underline the words in a that the pronouns replace.

1 a Stimson stood in the corner of his office staring at the young man.
   b "(He) must stop making eyes at Lizzie."

2 a The sign was huge. Each letter was six feet tall.
   b It glowed with light and could be seen from three blocks away.

3 a There was a circle of animals – lions, giraffes, camels, and horses.
   b They were painted in bright colors and shined in the mirrors in the center of the merry-go-round.

4 a The relationship between these two young people continued in silence.
   b They communicated with smiles and stares.

5 a . . . Lizzie's friend Jennie came over to the ticket booth and asked Lizzie if she wanted to walk along the beach after work.
   b Frank saw them talking . . .

6 a At first Frank was afraid to approach the girls because he remembered Stimson's warning.

   b He was a coward, but then he found the courage to get closer.

7 a "Jennie's really nice," said Lizzie.

   b "Yes, she is," Frank agreed.

8 a Frank looked at Lizzie and knew he was falling in love with her.

   b They held hands and walked back along the beach.

9 a Stimson always told his wife what to do . . .

   b . . . and she always obeyed.

10 a The young couple with the energy of youth flew ahead.

   b They had the power of dreams.

D THINKING CRITICALLY

1 Discussing the Story

With a partner or in a small group, discuss the following questions:

1 Why do you think Mr. Stimson does not like Frank and Lizzie's relationship?
2 Do you like Mr. Stimson? Why or why not?
3 Why does Jennie decide not to continue on the walk with Frank and Lizzie?
4 How do you think Mr. Stimson feels at the end of the story?
5 Are you glad that Mr. Stimson could not catch up with Frank and Lizzie? Why or why not?

2 Making Inferences

Authors often write something that can have more than one meaning. You need to figure out what the author means. This is called making inferences. Read the following sentences from the story. Then circle the answer that shows the author's meaning. If you need help, look back at the story. Discuss your answers.

1 She didn't look at her father and just played with the money on the shelf in the ticket booth.
   a Lizzie was afraid of her father.
   b Lizzie was busy selling tickets.
   c Lizzie was happy and was thinking of Frank.

2 After a while, Jennie said, "I'd like to sit here and look at the sea. You two go on. I'll catch up with you later."
   a Jennie is very tired and wants to rest.
   b Jennie wants Lizzie and Frank to be alone together.
   c Jennie is sad that Frank likes Lizzie.

3 Stimson always told his wife what to do, and she always obeyed. But this time she said, "No, John, not the rifle."
   a Stimson's wife is afraid her husband will kill the young couple.
   b Stimson's wife doesn't want to obey her husband anymore.
   c Stimson's wife wants her husband to hurt the couple, but not kill them.

4 He was just a powerless old man.
   a Stimson did not have the energy and passion of youth.
   b Stimson suddenly became old.
   c Stimson lost his power over other people.

3 Analyzing the Story: Theme

As you read on page 72, the theme of a story gives the author's opinion about life. But remember, the author doesn't tell you the theme; you must find it from the words in the story.

One theme for "The Pace of Youth" is "Love is powerful." One example from the story that matches this theme is in the chart below. Find two more examples in the story that match this theme and put them in the chart.

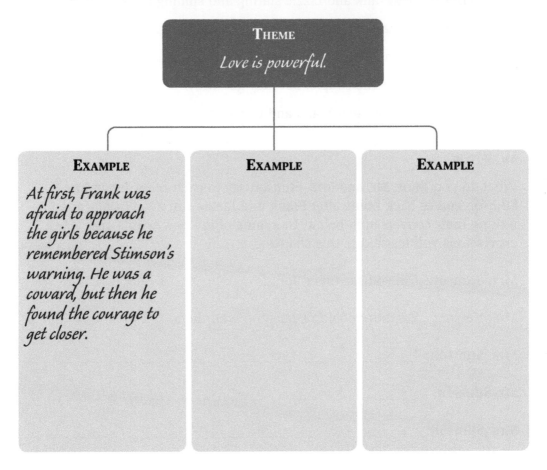

THEME

Love is powerful.

EXAMPLE

At first, Frank was afraid to approach the girls because he remembered Stimson's warning. He was a coward, but then he found the courage to get closer.

EXAMPLE

EXAMPLE

A story may have more than one theme. Find another theme from the story and make a chart like the one above. Share your charts with a partner.

4 Summarizing

Put the following sentences in the correct order to summarize the story. Write the numbers 1 to 6 to show the order. The first one has been done for you.

_____ Stimson tells Frank he'll fire him if he doesn't stop looking at his daughter.

_1_ Stimson sees Frank and Lizzie staring and smiling at each other.

_____ Frank and Lizzie walk on the beach and realize they're in love.

_____ When Stimson goes to his house, he finds his wife crying.

_____ Stimson chases the couple, but they get away.

_____ Stimson finds out that Frank and Lizzie ran away.

5 Writing

What do you think Mr. and Mrs. Stimson say to each other when Mr. Stimson comes back home after Frank and Lizzie run away? Continue writing their conversation below. Use some of the new words and expressions you learned in this chapter.

Mrs. Stimson: Did you see them, John?

Mr. Stimson: Yes, but I couldn't catch up with them.

Mrs. Stimson: _____

Mr. Stimson: _____

Mrs. Stimson: _____

Mr. Stimson: _____

Mrs. Stimson: _____

Mr. Stimson: _____

A TAKE A CLOSER LOOK

1 Theme Comparison: The Role of Fate

Some people believe that although we make plans for the future, fate actually controls our lives and what happens in them. All three stories in Part Two deal with the role of fate. All of the characters have experiences that control their futures, and as each story ends, we understand their fate.

With a partner, discuss the following questions.

1 What forces change the fate of Widow Buxton, Nehemiah Westfield, David Swan, Lizzie, Frank, and Mr. Stimson?
2 How would the stories end if fate did not enter the lives of the characters?
3 How do the characters act after fate changes their plans?

2 Freewriting

Write the word *fate* on the top of a sheet of paper. Then write any words that come into your mind when you think of fate. For 15 minutes, write about your own life. Do you remember a time or situation that was changed by fate? How did your life change? What did you think about at the time? How do you feel about it now?

B REVIEW

1 Grammar Review

Rewrite the following paragraph on a sheet of paper. Change the underlined words to the correct *count nouns, noncount nouns, articles,* and *pronouns.*

In a first story of Part Two, the Widow Buxton is dying. She asked the Nehemiah, a grave-diggers, to bury her cheaply. Her doesn't want to spend a lot of monies. Nehemiah insulted she. She attacked him and scared he so much that he died. In the second stories, David Swan falls asleep under the tree. A young girl stops by and looks at he. The David wakes up and never knows a events that happened to her. In a final story, two young lover run away together. A father of the girl is very angry, but she is old and tired and knows he must let they go.

2 Vocabulary Review

The definitions under Across and Down are for vocabulary words in Part Two. Read the definitions and complete the crossword puzzle with the correct vocabulary words.

Across

2 Do what someone tells you to do
5 When someone is brave they show this
6 A ceremony for a dead person
10 The way someone acts
14 A person who is traveling
15 Act as if something is true when it is not
16 Good, kind, not guilty
17 Send a message through behavior, writing, speaking, or art

Down

1 Two people or things together
3 Put something or someone into the ground
4 A place where dead people are buried
7 Foolish words or actions
8 Not knowing
9 A box that holds a dead person for a funeral or burial
11 Came near
12 Good looking
13 People who attend a funeral

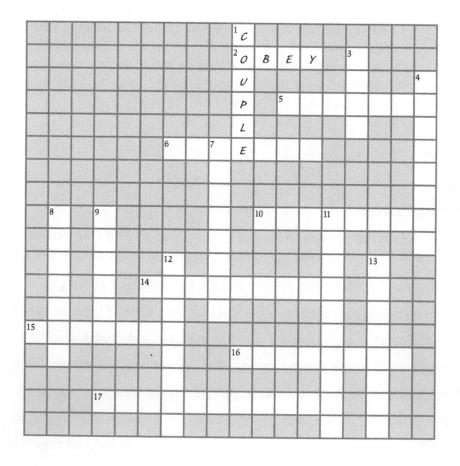

C ELEMENTS OF A SHORT STORY

Filling Out the Elements Chart

This chart shows the five basic elements of a short story. You can find definitions for these elements on page 170. Some of these elements have been filled out for "Omit Flowers." Complete the chart. Then copy the blank chart on page xvi and fill it out for "David Swan" or "The Pace of Youth" or for both stories. Share your charts with a partner or in a small group.

Elements of _____ *Omit Flowers* _____
(name of story)

SETTING

CHARACTERS

PLOT
An old woman and an old man have been angry at each other for many years. The woman hates the man because he left her on their wedding day. She finally gets her revenge when everyone thinks she is dying.

CONFLICT
The conflict is between Nehemiah Westfield and Widow Buxton who dislike each other.

THEME(S)
Hate is a powerful emotion that can affect people's lives. Another theme is "Beware the anger of a jilted woman."

WEBQUEST

Find more information about the topics in Part Two by going on the Internet. Go to www.cambridge.org/discoveringfiction/wq and follow the instructions for doing a WebQuest. Have fun. Enjoy the quest!

Mystery and Fantasy

MOST OF US like to read about strange events, and sometimes we even like to be scared. That is why mystery and fantasy are so popular in literature. As readers, we try to understand the truth of a story – what is real and what is fiction. As we read these stories, we love to try to figure out what is really happening in the story and why it is happening. We also try to figure out what will happen to the characters.

As you read the stories in Part Three, try to solve the mysteries in them. When will the wife of a lonely Californian man return home after visiting her family? Who are the strange people next door? What really happens to the school teacher in Sleepy Hollow?

CHAPTER 7

The Californian's Tale

MARK TWAIN

A PREPARING TO READ

1 Think Before You Read

Answer the following questions:

1 In 1849, gold was discovered in California. Men came from near and far to work in mining camps. Did the men live with their families? Do you think these men were lonely?
2 If a miner were married, what would be the difficulties?
3 What do you think homes were like in the small towns and miner camps in California?

2 Picture Focus

With a partner, talk about the picture. Where are the two men? What are they talking about?

3 Words to Know

Study the following key words and expressions from the story. They all relate to *a home and its contents*. Then complete the paragraph using each word or expression once.

log cabins small houses built with logs from trees	**cozy** warm and comfortable
cottages small houses	**washstand** a wooden piece of furniture used as a sink
decorated added things to a place to make it look nice	**towel** a cloth used to dry something that is wet
a woman's touch the style a woman puts in a house	

During the Gold Rush days, men lived in simple _____ _____ near rivers and streams. Later, as the men got married and started families, they often built small houses closer to town. These small houses were called _____. They often had flowers and gardens, and the women _____ them nicely. However, these small houses did not have running water inside. Instead, people usually had a wooden _____ with a bowl on top, and they put this in their bedrooms. People washed their hands and face in the bowl. A _____ hung on a bar nearby. These small houses could be very _____, especially with _____ _____ _____.

4 Story Preview

Read the preview of the story. Then answer the question in Making Predictions on the next page.

A young man meets an older man named Henry. Henry lives in a lovely cottage. Henry has a young wife who is away visiting her family. The young man sees a photo of the wife and wants to meet her. He agrees to stay with Henry for a few days to meet Henry's wife when she returns home.

5 Making Predictions

From the Story Preview, try to predict what will happen. Circle one choice below or write your own answer. Discuss your prediction with a partner.

What will happen when Henry's wife returns?

1 The young man will fall in love with her.

2 Henry's wife will tell the young man where to find gold.

3 Henry's wife will not return home.

4 _____

6 Idioms and Expressions

You will find these idioms and expressions in the story:

dropped by visited	**felt sorry for someone** felt sad for someone else's unhappiness
sent regards sent good wishes; said "hello"	**take turns** do something one person at a time
check your watch look at the time on your watch	**keep someone company** stay with someone, especially someone who is lonely

7 Literary Term: Surprise Ending

Some stories have a **surprise ending**. The ending can be sudden and unexpected. When you read the story, you expect it to end one way, but the writer surprises you with a different ending. Then if you read the story again, you can often find sentences that give you a clue* about the ending.

Focus As you read the story, think of how you expect the story to end. Are you surprised at the end? After you read the story, read it again. Notice which sentences in the story give you a clue about the ending.

* **clue:** information that helps you find an answer, solve a problem, or understand something

About the Author

Mark Twain (1835–1910) was born Samuel Clemens in Florida, Missouri. Mark Twain is the name Samuel Clemens used when he wrote stories. Twain is one of America's best-loved writers. His sense of humor and imagination helped make him famous as a writer and a speaker. He traveled all over the United States and the world talking to people.

Twain often wrote about life in the South in the 1800s. He used realistic characters and dialogue to tell his stories about intolerance[1] and friendship. Two of his most famous novels are *The Adventures of Tom Sawyer* and *The Adventures of Huckleberry Finn*. These books have been translated into many languages.

The Californian's Tale

I was mining in California, and I hoped to find gold. The weeks and months passed, and I never found my fortune.

It was beautiful out there, but very lonely. I used to live in a city, but now I saw only fields and trees and once in a while, an old log cabin.
5 When the easy gold was gone, almost everyone left. I was alone for a long time. And although I liked the peace and quiet, I was happy to see another human. He was a man about forty-five years old. He was standing next to a rose-covered cottage. The front yard was filled with flowers. His name was Henry, and he invited me into his cottage.
10 I thanked him and was happy to see his lovely home. The cottage was decorated with a woman's touch. There were pictures hanging on the walls and rugs on the floors. There were books, vases, and other pretty decorations. His cottage was very cozy. After living in a tent for many months, this was a wonderful change. He saw me smiling as I sat in a
15 wooden chair.

"It's all her work," he said with a loving voice. I watched him smooth a scarf which lay over the arm of a chair. It was like the pats a mother

---

[1]**intolerance**: not accepting other people's race, religion, customs, or ideas

gives a child after she combs and brushes the child's hair. "She always does that. I see her fix all these things so often that I can do it the way she does."

He took me into the bedroom so I could wash my hands. In the corner there was a washstand. I looked around the room, and once again I saw all the touches of a woman's taste. The towels were clean and white, and the soap sat in a floral soap dish. He kept smiling at me as I washed my hands and dried them with a towel.

Henry looked at me, and then he looked at a small photo sitting on a shelf. It was the photo of a beautiful, young woman.

"Is that your wife?" I asked.

"Yes, she was nineteen on her last birthday."

"Where is she now? When will she return?"

"Oh, she's away. She went to visit her family. They live about fifty miles away. She left two weeks ago."

"When do you expect her back?"

"This is Wednesday. She'll be back on Saturday at about nine o'clock at night."

"I'm sorry, I won't meet her because I have to leave before Saturday."

"Leave? Oh, she'll be so disappointed."

I looked at her photograph. I felt a deep, strong need to meet her.

"You see, she likes to have people come and stay with us. She likes to meet people who know things and can talk. She knows a lot and reads books. She'll be so disappointed. Please stay. It's only a few days from now. Please stay until Saturday."

Henry picked up the photograph and handed it to me.

"There now, tell her to her face that you can't stay to meet her."

When I looked at her face a second time, I knew I would stay. "Okay, my friend. I'll stay and meet your lovely wife."

We talked that night mostly about her. The next day was Thursday, and in the evening, an old miner dropped by for a visit. "I came by to ask about your wife, Henry. When is she coming home? Did you hear from her?"

"Oh yes, I received a letter. Would you like to hear it, Tom?"

"Sure, Henry."

Henry took the letter out of his wallet and read it to us. At the end of the letter, she sent regards to

Tom, Joe, and Charley, and some other neighbors. As Henry finished reading the letter, he said, "Tom, you are doing it again. Take your hands away from your eyes. You always do that when I read a letter from her. I'll tell her when she comes back."

"Oh no, Henry, I'm getting old, you know, and any disappointment makes me cry. I thought she'd be here herself, and now there's just a letter."

"Tom, everyone knows she's coming back on Saturday."

"Yes, Henry. I guess I did know that, but I forgot. I'll be sure to come back on Saturday." Tom said goodnight to us and left.

On Friday another old man came to visit from his cabin about a mile away. His name was Joe, and he said he and some of the other neighbors would come on Saturday to celebrate her return. Once again, Henry read her letter, and once again I saw tears in another old man's eyes.

Finally, on Saturday I kept looking at my watch while waiting for her to arrive. Henry noticed and said, "You're not worried about her are you?"

"No," I answered. "I always check my watch when I expect someone."

Four times Henry walked up the road and looked for her. "I'm worried," he said. "I know she's not due until nine o'clock, but maybe something happened. You don't think anything happened, do you?"

I hardly knew the man, but I felt sorry for him. He seemed like a child. I was glad when another friend, Charley, arrived at the house. He began talking to Henry. "Now you know nothing has happened. Why don't you go inside and take a nap so you'll be wide awake when she arrives?" Henry went into the bedroom.

It was then that I said to Charley, "Please stay here with me. She doesn't know me. We've never met, and I only stayed because it seemed so important to Henry. If Henry's sleeping, I don't want her to be uncomfortable to see a stranger."

"You won't be meeting her, young man. She's been missing for nineteen years. Yes, she was only nineteen when she went to visit her family. She never arrived home that night. The horse came home without her. We searched the woods for weeks, but there was no sign of her.

"Henry's never been the same. He does all right during the year, but as the anniversary of her disappearance approaches, we all take turns being with him. On the actual day, Tom, Joe, and I always come to be with him. We decorate the house with flowers and help Henry get through the day. There used to be a lot more of us in the early years, but we're getting old. Now there are just the three of us. Joe and Tom will be here soon. We'll sing some songs and keep him company until he falls asleep. We stay with him all night. Tomorrow he'll be okay and just remember his beautiful young wife. She sure was a lovely young woman. We all miss her."

UNDERSTANDING THE STORY

1 Reading Comprehension

With a partner or in a small group, discuss the following questions:

1 How does the young man meet Henry?
2 In what ways does Henry's house show "a woman's touch"?
3 How do Henry's friends behave when they visit him?
4 What does the young man learn about Henry's wife at the end of the story?

2 Guessing Meaning from Context

The words in the list are in the story. Find the words in the story. They are not listed in order. Try to understand their meanings. Then read the paragraph below. Replace the words in parentheses with words from the box. Use each word once.

human	anniversary	disappointed	invites
tears	expects	celebrate	disappearance
tent	taste	floral	scarf

The narrator of the story, a young man, lives alone in a (moveable house that is made of cloth) _____*tent*_____ outside the city. He never sees another (person) _____, but one day he meets Henry. Henry lives in a cozy cottage, and he (asks) _____ the young man to visit him. The cottage has flowers outside and (flowered) _____ dishes inside. The decorations show good (ability to enjoy and use beautiful things) _____. He watches Henry smooth a (piece of pretty cloth) _____ that is on a chair.

Later in the story, the young man says he plans to leave before Saturday. Henry is (very unhappy) _____ because he wants the young man to meet his wife. Henry (waits for) _____ his wife to come home on Saturday. The young man sees a photograph of Henry's wife and decides to stay.

Henry's friends come to visit. When Henry reads them a letter from his wife, the men have (drops of water) _____ in their eyes.

At the end of the story, the young man learns about the wife's (failure to return home) _____. He is surprised to hear that this happened 19 years ago. Henry's friends tell the young man that every year on the (date) _____ of this event, Henry's friends help him to (have a party for) _____ her return.

3 Grammar: Simple Present and Present Continuous Verb Tenses

Two present verb tense forms in English are the simple present and the present continuous.

● The simple present is used when a thing or an action is true or repeated. Words and phrases like *every day, every year, always, often, usually, sometimes,* or *never* can be used to show the simple present.

To make the simple present for singular subjects or the pronouns *he, she,* or *it,* add *-s, -es,* or *-ies* to the end of the main verb.

Examples:
Henry **tries** to keep his cottage clean.
Henry **misses** his wife.
Every day, Henry **waits** for his wife.

To make the simple present for plural subjects or the pronouns *I, you, we,* or *they,* do not add anything to the end of the main verb.

Examples:
Henry's friends **decorate** his house with flowers every year.
Tom, Joe, and Charley **keep** Henry company.
They **stay** with him all night.

continued

> ● The present continuous is used when an action is happening right now. Words like *now*, *right now*, or *at this moment* can be used to show the present continuous.
>
> To make the present continuous, use *is, am,* or *are* (forms of the auxiliary verb *be*) and the *-ing* form of the main verb.
>
> *Examples:*
> Right now, Henry **is waiting** for his wife.
> His friends **are waiting** with him.
> I **am waiting**, too.

Application 1   Look at the following sentences. In the chart next to the sentences, check ✓ *simple present* or *present continuous* for the verbs in **bold**.

	SIMPLE PRESENT	PRESENT CONTINUOUS
1 The young man **is looking** for gold today.	___	✓
2 In the story, the young man **meets** Henry.	___	___
3 Henry and the young man **go** into the cottage.	___	___
4 Henry **is showing** the young man his wife's picture now.	___	___
5 He **asks** the young man to stay and meet his wife.	___	___
6 The young man **decides** to stay until Saturday.	___	___
7 Now a neighbor **is reading** a letter from Henry's wife.	___	___
8 Some friends always **visit** Henry at this time of year.	___	___
9 Henry **waits** for his wife every day.	___	___
10 The men **are celebrating** at Henry's house at this moment.	___	___

Application 2   In the following sentences, look at the underlined verb or verbs. If the verb form is correct, put a check ✓ next to the sentence. If the verb form is incorrect, write the correct sentence on the blank line.

1 Every anniversary, Henry's friends <u>are staying</u> with him.

   Every anniversary, Henry's friends stay with him.

2 They <u>decorate</u> his house for him.

   _____

3 Right now, the men <u>come</u> to Henry's house.

   _____

4 The men always <u>stay</u> with Henry all night.

   _____

5 Everyone usually <u>is singing</u> songs.

   _____

6 Henry often <u>falls</u> asleep during the celebration.

   _____

7 When he wakes up, Henry <u>is</u> always <u>remembering</u> his lovely wife.

   _____

8 All the men <u>are missing</u> Henry's wife.

   _____

D THINKING CRITICALLY

1 Discussing the Story

With a partner or in a small group, discuss the following questions:

1 In the beginning of the story, did you notice anything strange about Henry's behavior? Explain your answer.
2 Why does the young man decide to stay and meet Henry's wife?
3 Does the friendship of the other men help or hurt Henry? Why or why not?
4 What do you think happened to Henry's wife? Why didn't she return home?

2 Making Inferences

Authors often write something that can have more than one meaning. You need to figure out what the author means. This is called making inferences. Read the following sentences from the story. Then circle the answer that shows the author's meaning. If you need help, look back at the story. Discuss your answers.

1 I watched him smooth a scarf which lay over the arm of a chair. It was like the pats a mother gives a child after she combs and brushes the child's hair.
   a Henry smoothed the scarf the way a mother smoothes her child's hair.
   b Henry loved and missed his wife.
   c Henry thought his house needed to be cleaned.

2 Henry looked at me, and then he looked at a small photo sitting on a shelf.
   a Henry did not want to look at the young man anymore.
   b Henry wanted the young man to notice the photo.
   c Henry wanted the young man to leave.

3 Once again, Henry read her letter, and once again I saw tears in another old man's eyes.
   a Something about the letter made the old men cry.
   b Another old man had something in his eyes.
   c Henry read the letter too many times, and the old men were bored.

3 Analyzing the Story: Surprise Ending

As you read on page 90, many stories have surprise endings. If you read the story again, you will see that some sentences in the story give clues about the ending. Put a check ✓ next to the sentences below that are clues. Put an X next to the sentences that are not clues.

SETTING	CLUES	NOT CLUES
The cottage was decorated with a woman's touch. There were pictures hanging on the walls and rugs on the floors. There were books, vases, and other pretty decorations.		X
"Yes, she was nineteen on her last birthday."		
"Tom, you are doing it again. Take your hands away from your eyes. You always do that when I read a letter from her."		
Four times Henry walked up the road and looked for her. "I'm worried," he said. "I know she's not due until nine o'clock, but maybe something happened. You don't think anything happened, do you?"		

4 Summarizing

Put the following sentences in the correct order to summarize the story. Write the numbers 1 to 6 to show the order. The first one has been done for you.

_____ Henry is waiting for his wife to return from a visit to her family.

_____ Each neighbor drops by to see when she will return.

_____ Henry reads a letter from his wife, and the neighbors cry.

_____ Henry shows the young man a picture of his wife.

_____ The young man learns that Henry's wife disappeared 19 years ago.

_1_ Henry invites the young man to come into his cozy cottage.

5 Writing

Pretend you are Henry's young wife. Write a letter telling him what you are doing now and what you do every day while visiting your family. Use the present verb tenses.

CHAPTER 8

Rain, Rain, Go Away

Isaac Asimov

A PREPARING TO READ

1 Think Before You Read

Answer the following questions:

1 What do people like to do when the weather is sunny?
2 What do people do when the weather is rainy?
3 What is your favorite weather? Why?

2 Picture Focus

With a partner, talk about the picture. What is the weather like in the picture, and where are the people going?

3 Words to Know

Study the following key words from the story. They all relate to *weather*. Then complete the paragraph using each word once.

cloudy not a clear, sunny day; clouds cover the sky	**barometer** a device that shows if it will be rainy or sunny
forecast an official prediction of what kind of weather to expect	**stormy** a kind of weather with thunder, lightning, and rain
fair a clear day with nice weather; not cloudy	**thundershowers** very heavy rain

An important part of the daily news is the weather _____. If you have plans to be outside, you will want to know if it will be sunny or not. If the newspaper has a picture of a cloud, it will be a _____ day. Sometimes, the prediction may promise _____ weather, and so you don't expect rain. However, when you go out and see a dark, _____ sky, you know there will be _____ and lightning. If you look at your _____ and it shows it will rain, you should spend the day indoors.

4 Story Preview

Read the preview of the story. Then answer the question in Making Predictions on the next page.

Lillian Wright is very curious about her new neighbors, the Sakkaros. No one knows what Mr. Sakkaro does for a job, and Mrs. Sakkaro is always looking at the sky. They never go out when it is cloudy. One day Mrs. Wright invites the Sakkaros to join her family and spend the day at Murphy's Park. The Sakkaros agree to go as long as it is fair weather.

5 Making Predictions

From the Story Preview, try to predict what will happen. Circle one choice below or write your own answer. Discuss your prediction with a partner.

What will happen at Murphy's Park?

1 Mr. Sakkaro will tell the Wrights what he does for a living.

2 The Sakkaros will want to go home.

3 The Sakkaros will explain why they don't go out when it's cloudy.

4 _____

6 Idioms and Expressions

You will find these idioms and expressions in the story:

keep to themselves are very private people	**fill up on** eat a lot of one kind of food and not want to eat anything else
does for a living what someone's job is	
called up telephoned someone	**piped up** spoke up to be heard
turn green feel very nauseous	**sprung up** suddenly appeared
sicken on the spot suddenly vomit	

7 Literary Term: Atmosphere

Atmosphere is the feelings or mood a story creates. The author often uses the setting or events to create a pleasant or unpleasant atmosphere. Isaac Asimov often wrote about different worlds or alternative realities. Sometimes these differences created a feeling or mood of fear and horror.

Focus   As you read the story, notice how your feelings change from the beginning to the end of the story. At what point does your mood change?

THE STORY

About the Author

Isaac Asimov (1920–1998) was born in Russia but grew up in the United States. He graduated with honors from Columbia University in 1948 with a doctorate degree in biochemistry. In 1949, Asimov became a professor of biochemistry at Boston University. Asimov wrote and edited more than 500 books and an estimated 90,000 letters and postcards. Much of his work was about science and the history of science, for which he received several awards. However, he is best known for his science fiction novels and short stories. He also wrote several popular novels, such as *I Robot* (1950), and *The Robots of Dawn* (1983). He even wrote a series of adventure stories for young people, entitled "The Lucky Star," in which a space ranger was the hero.

Rain, Rain, Go Away

"There she is again, George" said Lillian Wright as she looked out the window.

"Who?" asked her husband, trying to watch the baseball game on TV.

"Mrs. Sakkaro," she said. "The new neighbor."

5 "Oh."

"I wonder where her boy is. He's a *nice* boy. I wish Tommie would make friends with him. It's hard with the Sakkaros. They keep to themselves. I don't even know what Mr. Sakkaro does for a living."

"Mrs. Sakkaro knows what Mr. Sakkaro does for a living. Maybe she's 10 upset because she doesn't know what *I* do."

"Oh, George." Lillian glanced with distaste at the television. "I think we should make an effort to be friendly, but she's so odd. She's always looking at the sky, and she's never been out when it's the least bit cloudy. Once, when the boy was out playing, she had him come in, shouting that 15 it was going to rain. But it was perfectly sunny."

"Did it rain, eventually?"

"Of course not."

Lillian went back to the window and said, "Oh, look at that, George."
George looked at nothing but the TV.

20   Lillian said, "I know she's staring at that cloud."
Two days later, Lillian told George excitedly, "We're going out with the Sakkaros to Murphy's Park."
"How did it happen?"
"I just went up to their house this morning and rang the bell."

25   "That easy?"
"It wasn't easy. It was hard. I stood there, jittering, with my finger on the doorbell."
"And she didn't kick you out?"
"No. She invited me in and said she was so glad I had come."

30   "Did she agree to come with us right away?"
"Well – not right away. She asked her husband what the weather forecast was, and he said that the newspapers all said it would be fair tomorrow."
"All the newspapers said so, eh?"

35   "I think they get all the newspapers. At least I've watched the bundle the newsboy leaves. Anyway, she called up the weather bureau and had them give her the latest report. She said they'd go, unless there were any unexpected changes in the weather."
"All right. Then we'll go."

40   The Sakkaros were young and handsome. As they walked to the Wright's car, George leaned toward his wife and whispered, "So *he*'s the reason you are so interested in them."
"I wish he were," said Lillian. "Is that a handbag he's carrying?"
"Pocket-radio. To listen to weather forecasts, I bet."

45   The Sakkaro boy followed. He carried a barometer. All three got into the back seat.
It was a beautiful day at Murphy's Park. Lillian took the two boys to the amusement section and bought tickets to every ride.
When she returned, George was alone. "Where –" she began.

50   "At the refreshment stand. I told them I'd wait for you and we would join them." He sounded gloomy.
"Anything wrong?"
"No, except that I think he must be independently wealthy."
"What?"

55   "I don't know what he does for a living. He said he's just a student of human nature."
"That would explain all those newspapers."
"Yes, but with a handsome, wealthy man next door, it looks as though I'll have impossible standards set for me."

60   "Don't be silly."
"Come on, they're waving. Oh, look what they've bought."

The Sakkaros were each holding three sticks of cotton candy, huge swirls of pink threads of sugar dried out of syrup. It melted sweetly in the mouth and left one feeling sticky.

65 The Sakkaros held one out to each Wright, and the Wrights accepted. The adults played darts[1] and a poker[2] game. The boys went on more rides. The Sakkaros ate several more cotton candy sticks.

George and Lillian walked slowly behind the group. "If I see them eat another cotton candy stick," said George, "I'll turn green and sicken on 70 the spot. They've had a dozen[3] each!"

"I suppose they've never had cotton candy before and they need to adjust to the novelty. They'll fill up on it and then never eat it again."

"Well, maybe." They strolled toward the Sakkaros. "You know, Lil, it's clouding up."

75 Suddenly, all three Sakkaros ran to George and begged to go home. It looked stormy.

Mrs. Sakkaro wailed that all the forecasts had been for fair weather.

George tried to console them. "Even if a storm were to come, it wouldn't last more than half an hour."

80 The drive back seemed very long. There was no conversation. Mr. Sakkaro's radio was quite loud. Weather reports mentioned "local thundershowers."

The Sakkaro youngster piped up that the barometer was falling, and Mrs. Sakkaro stared at the sky.

85 "It does look threatening, doesn't it?" Lillian said to be polite. But then George heard her mutter quietly, "It's only a little bit of rain!"

A wind had sprung up when they entered their street and the leaves rustled ominously.

George said, "You'll be indoors in two minutes, friends. We'll make 90 it."

He pulled up to the Sakkaros's house. The Sakkaros got out, faces filled with tension, and ran toward their door.

"Honestly," said Lillian, "you would think they were –"

Halfway to their door, the rain started. The Sakkaros stopped and 95 looked up despairingly. As the drops hit, their faces blurred and shrank. All three shriveled and sank down into three sticky-wet heaps.

The Wrights stared with horror. Lillian completed her remark: "– made of sugar and afraid they would melt."

---

[1]**darts**: a game where small pointed arrows are thrown at a circular board
[2]**poker**: a game played with cards where people try to win money from each other
[3]**a dozen**: twelve of something

C UNDERSTANDING THE STORY

1 Reading Comprehension

With a partner or in a small group, discuss the following questions:

1 Why is Lillian Wright curious about her neighbors, the Sakkaros?
2 Where does she invite them to go with her family?
3 What do the Sakkaros bring with them?
4 Why do they want to go home suddenly?
5 What happens to the Sakkaros?

2 Guessing Meaning from Context

The words in the list are in the story. Find the words in the story, and try to understand their meanings. Match each word to the correct definition on the right. Write the letter of the definition on the blank line.

_h_	1	odd	**a** many things tied together
___	2	eventually	**b** something new
___	3	jittering	**c** good-looking
___	4	handsome	**d** finally, a later time
___	5	bundle	**e** made a loud, sad cry
___	6	novelty	**f** get smaller and weaker
___	7	wailed	**g** in a threatening way
___	8	console	**h** different; strange
___	9	ominously	**i** making small nervous movements
___	10	tension	**j** anxiety
___	11	shriveled	**k** show understanding of feelings; sympathy
___	12	despairingly	**l** with a feeling of no hope that a bad situation will improve

3 Grammar: The Simple Past Tense and Regular and Irregular Verb Forms

The simple past tense shows that an action happened in the past and is finished. In English, the simple past is formed by changing regular verbs and irregular verbs.

- To make the simple past of regular verbs, add *-d* or *-ed* to the end.

Examples:
imagine → imagined   adjust → adjusted   ask → asked

When a verb ends in *y*, and *y* is a vowel sound, change the *y* to *i* and add *-ed*.

Examples:
carry → carried   dry → dried   try→ tried

When a verb has a short vowel followed by a consonant, double the consonant and add *-ed*.

Examples:
drop → dropped   grab → grabbed   stop → stopped

- To make the simple past of irregular verbs, you must memorize their forms.

Examples:
is / am / are → was / were
have / has → had

begin → began	come → came	get → got
go → went	hear → heard	know → knew
make → made	run → ran	say → said
shrink → shrank	sink → sank	see → saw
spring → sprung	take → took	wear → wore

Note that some irregular verbs have the same form in the present and past tenses.
put → put   set → set   hit → hit

Application 1   Reread the last few paragraphs from the story (lines 80 to 98) and find five regular past tense verbs and five irregular past tense verbs. Then fill in the chart below by putting the verbs in the correct columns.

REGULAR PAST TENSE	IRREGULAR PAST TENSE
seemed	*was*

Application 2   The following sentences are about the story. Complete each sentence with the correct past tense form of the verb in parentheses.

1 When the weather was cloudy, Mrs. Sakkaro never _____*went*_____ (go) outside.

2 When it _____ (be) sunny, Mrs. Sakkaro _____ (look) at the sky to check for clouds.

3 When Mrs. Wright _____ (invite) the Sakkaros to Murphy Park, they _____ (bring) a pocket-radio to listen to weather forecasts.

4 At the park, the Sakkaros _____ (eat) a lot of cotton candy.

5 The boys _____ (go) on lots of different amusement rides at the park, and their parents _____ (play) games, such as darts and a kind of poker.

6 It _____ (be) a beautiful day until some clouds _____ (appear) and a wind _____ (spring) up.

7 Everyone _____ (see) the sky looked stormy, and George Wright _____ (tell) the Sakkaros that the storm would not last long.

8 The Sakkaros _____ (beg) the Wrights to take them home immediately.

9 George Wright _____ (say) they would make it but, when they _____ (reach) the Sakkaros's house, the rain _____ (start).

10 The Sakkaros _____ (get) so wet that they _____ (sink) down into sticky heaps.

D THINKING CRITICALLY

1 Discussing the Story

With a partner or in a small group, discuss the following questions:

1 Why is the story told mainly through Lillian Wright's viewpoint?
2 Do you like or dislike Lillian? Give a reason for your opinion.
3 What part does her husband George play in the story?
4 Why do the Sakkaros agree to go on a day trip with the Wrights?
5 Where do you think the Sakkaros come from?

2 Making Inferences

Authors often write something that can have more than one meaning. You need to figure out what the author means. This is called making inferences. Read the following sentences from the story. Then circle the answer that shows the author's meaning. If you need help, look back at the story. Discuss your answers.

1 "Oh, George." Lillian glanced with distaste at the television.
  a She is angry that Tommie is not friends with the Sakkaro boy.
  b She is angry that her husband seems more interested in the TV program than what she is telling him about the neighbors.
  c She is angry that her husband does not know what Mr. Sakkaro's job is.

2 "Did she [Mrs. Sakkaro] agree to come with us right away?" "Well – not right away."

   a Mrs. Sakkaro didn't like Mrs. Wright and didn't want to join the Wrights.

   b Mrs. Sakkaro was busy listening to the weather forecast and didn't hear Mrs. Wright.

   c Mrs. Sakkaro wanted to know the weather forecast before she agreed to join the Wrights.

3 He sounded gloomy. "Anything wrong?" "No, except that I think he must be independently wealthy."

   a Mr. Wright wants to go home.

   b Mr. Wright is tired.

   c Mr. Wright is jealous of Mr. Sakkaro.

4 But then George heard her [Mrs. Wright] mutter quietly, "It's only a little bit of rain!"

   a Mrs. Wright is sympathetic toward the Sakkaros.

   b Mrs. Wright is irritated by the Sakkaros's behavior.

   c Mrs. Wright is worried that they will all get wet in the rain.

3 Analyzing the Story: Atmosphere

As you read, the atmosphere of a story makes you feel something pleasant or unpleasant. Until the weather turns cloudy at Murphy's Park, the atmosphere in the story you have just read is friendly and peaceful. When the first clouds appear in the sky, the Sakkaros beg George to take them home immediately. Note how the impending summer storm dramatically increases the feeling of tension during the ride home. The final feeling is one of horror.

Reread the last few paragraphs of the story and note how the effect of changes in nature changes the atmosphere. Find words and phrases that create this tense feeling. Write those items in the chart. One example has been done for you.

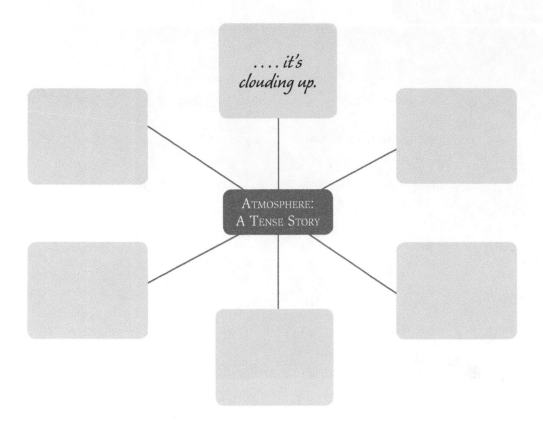

4 Summarizing

Put the following sentences in the correct order to summarize the story.
Write the numbers 1 to 7 to show the order. The first one has been done
for you.

____ The rain catches the Sakkaro family halfway to their door.

____ Lillian Wright invites the Sakkaros to Murphy's Park.

____ The Sakkaros melt into sticky-wet heaps.

____ The Sakkaros bring a pocket-radio and a barometer to the park.

_1_ Mrs. Wright remarks that her neighbors keep to themselves.

____ The Sakkaros eat only cotton candy at Murphy's Park.

____ At the first sign of rain, the Sakkaros beg George Wright to take them
home immediately.

5 Writing

A friend of Tommie asks him if he had a good time at Murphy's Park. Write
the dialogue between the two boys.

CHAPTER 9

The Legend of Sleepy Hollow

WASHINGTON IRVING

A PREPARING TO READ

1 Think Before You Read

Answer the following questions:

1 What does the word *legend* mean?
2 What are some legends from your culture? Explain one legend.
3 Do you believe legends can be true? Why or why not?

2 Picture Focus

With a partner, talk about the picture. Why does the man look frightened?

3 Words to Know

Study the following key words from the story. They all relate to *the supernatural*. Then complete the paragraph using each word once.

superstitious believing that certain things will bring bad luck	**tales** stories that are invented or hard to believe
ghosts the spirits of dead people that visit living people	**mysterious** describing something that cannot be explained
haunt appear somewhere, often in the form of a ghost	

The supernatural cannot be explained by our knowledge of science. However, some people believe in supernatural events. These people are very

_____. They may believe that legends and strange

_____ are true. In some cultures, people think that any Friday

that is on the thirteenth day of a month is an unlucky day. Other cultures

think that if they see the number 4, they will die. Some people also believe in

_____. They think that the spirits of the dead _____

certain places around us. Maybe these people read too many scary stories

about _____ events.

4 Story Preview

Read the preview of the story. Then answer the question in Making Predictions on the next page.

> The people of Sleepy Hollow are superstitious. They believe in ghosts, especially one they call the Headless Horseman. This ghost rides through the village at midnight looking for his head. Most of the townspeople are afraid of him, including Ichabod Crane, the village school teacher.

5 Making Predictions

From the Story Preview, try to predict what will happen. Circle one choice below or write your own answer. Discuss your prediction with a partner.

What will happen if Ichabod Crane meets the ghost?

1 Ichabod will try to kill the ghost.

2 Ichabod will leave Sleepy Hollow.

3 Ichabod will help the ghost find his head.

4 _____

6 Idioms and Expressions

You will find these idioms and expressions in the story:

play tricks on make another person the victim of a joke or bad event	**broke up** ended an event or a relationship
feasting on enjoying a lot of good food	**marriage proposal** the time when a person asks someone to marry him or her
mouth watering looks so good you can't wait to eat it	**goose bumps** small bumps that cover the skin when someone is frightened or cold

7 Literary Term: Foreshadowing

Foreshadowing is when an author gives you clues about what is going to happen in the story. You can find the clues easily as you read the story. In surprise endings (see Chapter 7, page 90), you often can't find the clues about the ending until you read the story a second time. Authors often use foreshadowing for mysteries and horror stories.

Focus   As you read the story, look for clues about what is going to happen to the main character, Ichabod Crane.

About the Author

Washington Irving (1783–1859) was born in New York City. He studied law for a short time, and then he decided to become a writer. He had success with his first book, *A History of New York*. About the same time, he became engaged to Matilda Hoffman. She died suddenly, and Irving was so sad that he never married. He went to Europe to forget the death of his fiancée, and he decided to live in Spain. In 1826, Irving went to work at the U.S. embassy in Madrid. In Europe, Irving wrote and published *The Sketch Book*. This book introduced the character Ichabod Crane in the story "The Legend of Sleepy Hollow."

Washington Irving later returned to the United States. He spent the rest of his life in Tarrytown, New York. There he built a home. He called it "Sunnyside." The house is now a museum dedicated to the memory of Washington Irving.

The Legend of Sleepy Hollow

Many years ago, there was a little town in the green valleys of the state of New York. The place was called Sleepy Hollow.

The people in this quiet village were very superstitious. They believed in ghosts. One particular ghost haunted the countryside. It was a ghost
5 riding on a horse, and the ghost did not have a head on its body. People said it was the ghost of a soldier from the Revolutionary War.[1] The soldier's head was shot off by a cannon ball.

So everyone called the ghost "The Headless Horseman of Sleepy Hollow." People said the soldier was buried in one of the graves at the

---

[1]**Revolutionary War**: the war in the 1700s that was fought between the American Colonies and England and that led to the colonies becoming the United States of America

10 church. They believed the Horseman rode to the battlefield every night, looking for his head.

There was only one teacher in Sleepy Hollow. His name was Ichabod Crane. He was not a good-looking man. He was very tall and thin. His head was small, but his ears were large and his nose was long. Ichabod
15 loved to eat. He didn't get much money working as a teacher, so he was always looking for a good meal. People often invited him to dinner. The women liked his good manners. He was a good source of news, and he taught singing.

Ichabod liked stories of ghosts. He enjoyed visiting the old women
20 in the village. They passed many evenings telling tales of ghosts. They told tales of haunted fields, haunted bridges, and haunted houses, and particularly of the Headless Horseman. Ichabod always had to walk home alone at night after hearing the scary stories.

Ichabod's other interest was young ladies. He was in love with pretty Katrina Van Tassel. She was the only daughter of a rich farmer. Ichabod decided to ask Katrina to marry him. However, another man, Brom Bones, wanted to marry her, too.

Brom was big and strong. He was a great horse rider. He liked to play tricks on people he didn't like. Brom was also jealous. He soon noticed Ichabod's interest in Katrina. Bad feelings grew between Brom and Ichabod. Brom Bones boasted about what he would do to Ichabod Crane.

One fall day, when Ichabod was teaching, a man came to the
40 schoolhouse with a letter. It was an invitation to a party at Van Tassel's farm. Ichabod was very excited. He quickly gave the students their lessons. He let them go home an hour early. Then he brushed his best coat and combed his hair. He borrowed an old horse and a saddle from Mr. Hans Van Ripper, to ride to the party.
45 It was evening when Ichabod arrived at Van Tassel's home. Everyone was feasting on all kinds of mouthwatering food. Ichabod was very happy while he was eating. He was thinking about the riches of Van Tassel's farm. He was thinking about asking Katrina to marry him. He was sure she would say yes. Then he would have a beautiful wife and
50 Van Tassel's farm.

> They passed many evenings telling tales of ghosts. They told tales of haunted fields, haunted bridges, and haunted houses, and particularly of the Headless Horseman.

Brom Bones was also at the party. He came on his favorite horse – an animal known for its speed. Brom was boasting about his horse when Ichabod came in.

A musician began to play. Soon people were dancing. Ichabod was dancing with Katrina. Ichabod was as proud of his dancing as he was of his singing. Brom Bones was watching jealously from the corner.

When the dance ended, Ichabod joined a group of older men and women. They were telling stories about ghosts and strange events. The stories turned to their favorite ghost – the Headless Horseman. They said that every night, the Horseman tied his horse to a tree among the graves at the church.

The men and women were also talking about Old Brouwer, a farmer who said he didn't believe in ghosts. One night, Brouwer met the Horseman on the road. The Horseman made Brouwer get on his horse behind him and ride with him. At the bridge next to the church, the Horseman threw Brouwer into the small river. With the sound of thunder, the Horseman rode off over the treetops. Brom boasted that one time he had a race with the ghost, and Brom almost won.

The party gradually broke up. The old farmers took their families home. The younger people, with their arms around each other, began to leave. Ichabod stayed behind to make his marriage proposal. But something must have gone wrong because a few minutes later, Ichabod ran out the front door of Van Tassel's home, ran straight to his horse, and rode toward his own home. The time was midnight.

The night grew darker. Ichabod thought of the stories about the Headless Horseman. He was coming to the wooden bridge when suddenly, he saw something large and black. Goose bumps covered Ichabod's body, and the hair on his head rose in fear. The figure had no head! It was the horseman, and he was carrying his head on his saddle. Ichabod kicked his horse to make it go faster, but the Headless Horseman rode right behind Ichabod.

Ichabod was not a good rider. The saddle became loose, and it fell to the ground. In his terror, Ichabod grabbed his horse's neck. If only he could get across the bridge! At that moment, the ghost took his head and threw it at Ichabod. The head hit Ichabod and knocked him off his horse.

The next morning, Van Ripper found his horse without its saddle. Ichabod did not appear at breakfast. The boys came to the school, but there was no teacher. Dinner time came, but where was Ichabod?

On the road someone found the saddle. On the wooden bridge were Ichabod Crane's hat and a broken pumpkin. The farmers searched the small river, but Ichabod's body was never found.

The mysterious event caused much talk among the people of Sleepy Hollow. They were sure that the Headless Horsemen carried Ichabod Crane away.

95 Several years later, a farmer from Sleepy Hollow visited New York City. He came back with the news that Ichabod Crane was alive. Ichabod said he left Sleepy Hollow out of fear of the ghost and because he was disappointed in love. Ichabod did well in the city. He became a lawyer, then a politician, and finally a judge.

100 Meanwhile, Brom Bones married Katrina Van Tassel. Brom always enjoyed hearing the story of Ichabod Crane. He laughed loudly every time someone mentioned the pumpkin.

The old country women, however, still believe that the ghost took Ichabod away on his midnight ride in Sleepy Hollow. People grew even
105 more superstitious about the bridge. They moved the road to the church to avoid the bridge, and they no longer used the old schoolhouse. Some people reported that the ghost of the unfortunate teacher haunted the empty schoolhouse. Others imagine hearing him singing in the peaceful valleys around Sleepy Hollow.

C UNDERSTANDING THE STORY

1 Reading Comprehension

With a partner or in a small group, discuss the following questions:

1 What do the people of Sleepy Hollow believe about the Headless Horseman?
2 What kind of man is Ichabod Crane? Describe him.
3 Why is Ichabod so happy to receive an invitation to the party at Van Tassel's home?
4 Why is Brom Bones jealous of Ichabod Crane?
5 What happens to Ichabod after he leaves the party at Van Tassel's farm?

2 Guessing Meaning from Context

The words in the list are in the story. Find the words in the story, and try to understand their meanings. Then complete the sentences with words in the list. Use each word once.

valley	soldier	buried	manners
boast	borrow	saddle	jealous
thunder	loose	pumpkin	search

1 Brom Bones liked to _____*boast*_____ about himself. He said he was the best at everything.

2 Ichabod Crane didn't have a horse. He had to _____ one.

3 Brom Bones was _____ of Ichabod Crane. Brom wanted to marry Katrina.

4 Ichabod also needed a _____ for the horse.

5 Everyone liked to invite Ichabod for dinner because he had nice _____.

6 Sleepy Hollow was in a beautiful _____ in the state of New York.

7 On the bridge, the men found a big orange _____. It was broken.

8 People said the Headless Horseman was the ghost of a _____.

9 The body was _____ in a grave near the church.

10 People heard _____ when the Headless Horseman flew over the trees.

11 The townspeople decided to _____ in the small river for Ichabod's body.

12 The saddle was _____ on the horse. Ichabod had to grab the horse's neck.

3 Grammar: Simple Past and Past Continuous Verb Tenses

Both the simple past tense and the past continuous tense are used for actions in the past. In Chapter 8 (page 107), you learned that the simple past is used for an action that happened in the past and is finished.

● The past continuous is used for an action in the past that is taking place just before another action in the past begins. We often use it in the same sentence as the simple past.

To make the past continuous verb tense, use *was* or *were* + the *-ing* form of the main verb.

Examples:

PAST CONTINUOUS   SIMPLE PAST

One fall day, while Ichabod **was teaching**, a man **came** to the schoolhouse with a letter.

● Some verbs are not usually used in the past continuous form.

Examples:

know	want	need	like	hear
love	hate	seem	believe	

Application 1   The following sentences are about the story. Circle the correct verb or verbs in parentheses to complete each sentence.

1 Ichabod (was planning / planning) to ask Katrina to marry him.

2 A lot of people (was dancing / were dancing) at the party.

3 Brom Bones (was watching / watching) while Ichabod (dance / was dancing) with Katrina.

4 Brom often (boasted / boasting) about what he (want / wanted) to do to Ichabod.

5 Katrina (was making / was made) Brom jealous.

6 Ichabod (went / going) to sit with some of the old men and women. The older people (were telling / was telling) ghost stories.

Application 2   Read the following conversation between two women in Sleepy Hollow. Next to each sentence in the chart, check ✓ simple past or past continuous for the verbs in bold.

	SIMPLE PRESENT	PRESENT CONTINUOUS
Anna: Hello, Betty. What **were** you **doing**?	____	✓
Betty: I **was cooking** dinner.	____	____
Anna: What **were** you **making**?	____	____
Betty: Soup. My brother **sent** me a chicken from his farm.	____	____
Anna: **Did** you **hear** the news?	____	____
Betty: What news? Nobody **told** me anything.	____	____
Anna: A horseman without a head **was riding** through	____	____
town last night, and someone **saw** him!	____	____
Betty: What **did** you **say**? No head? On a horse?	____	____
Was someone **imagining** things?	____	____

Anna: Well, old Brouwer **was walking** home last night when   ____   ____

the headless man **rode** by on his big, black horse.   ____   ____

Betty: So what **happened**?   ____   ____

Anna: The ghost **made** Brouwer get up on his horse!   ____   ____

Betty: But old Brouwer never **believed** in ghosts.   ____   ____

Anna: Well, he **changed** his mind last night!   ____   ____

D THINKING CRITICALLY

1 Discussing the Story

With a partner or in a small group, discuss the following questions:

1 Do you like Ichabod Crane? Why or why not?
2 Do you like Brom Bones? Why is he important in the story? Explain your answers.
3 Why does everyone fear the Headless Horseman?
4 What do you think happened when Ichabod asked Katrina to marry him?
5 Why do you think the people of Sleepy Hollow found a pumpkin on the wooden bridge?

2 Making Inferences

Authors often write something that can have more than one meaning. You need to figure out what the author means. This is called making inferences. Read the following sentences from the story. Then circle the answer that shows the author's meaning. If you need help, look back at the story. Discuss your answers.

1 He [Brom Bones] liked to play tricks on people he didn't like.
   a Brom Bones was a funny person.
   b Brom Bones loved Katrina.
   c Brom Bones didn't like Ichabod.

2 . . . suddenly, he saw something large and black.
  a It was the Headless Horseman.
  b It was a large tree.
  c It was the bridge over the stream.

3 Brom always enjoyed hearing the story of Ichabod Crane. He laughed loudly every time someone mentioned the pumpkin.
  a Brom didn't believe the story.
  b Brom knew a secret about the pumpkin.
  c Brom was glad that Ichabod left the village.

3 Analyzing the Story: Foreshadowing

As you read on page 114, foreshadowing is when an author gives clues about what is going to happen in the story. The end of "The Legend of Sleepy Hollow" is summarized in the box on the right. Find examples of foreshadowing in the story that help predict the ending. Find one example for each set of lines from the story. Put the examples in the boxes on the left.

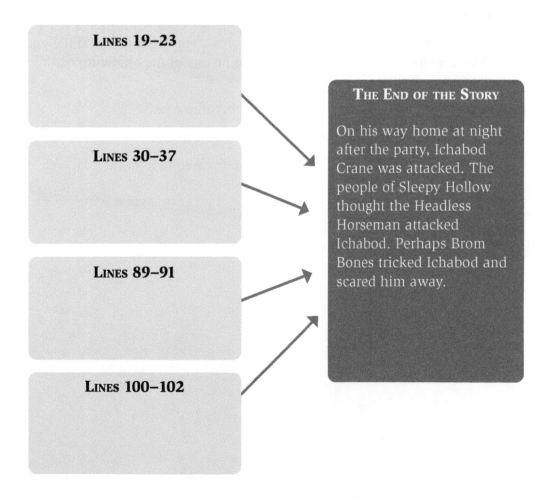

LINES 19–23

LINES 30–37

LINES 89–91

LINES 100–102

THE END OF THE STORY

On his way home at night after the party, Ichabod Crane was attacked. The people of Sleepy Hollow thought the Headless Horseman attacked Ichabod. Perhaps Brom Bones tricked Ichabod and scared him away.

4 Summarizing

Put the following sentences in the correct order to summarize the story. Write the numbers 1 to 8 to show the order. The first one has been done for you.

____ Ichabod Crane receives an invitation to Van Tassel's party.

____ Ichabod's hat and a broken pumpkin are found on the wooden bridge.

_1_ The people of Sleepy Hollow believe in ghosts.

____ The Headless Horseman chases Ichabod and knocks him off his horse.

____ Brom Bones marries Katrina.

____ People say the Headless Horseman is the ghost of a soldier.

____ At midnight, Ichabod leaves the party after something goes wrong.

____ Ichabod makes Brom Bones jealous.

5 Writing

Write a paragraph that explains what you think really happened at the end of "The Legend of Sleepy Hollow." It could be one of the following endings or your own choice.

• Ichabod ran away to New York City and became a judge.

• The Headless Horseman carried Ichabod Crane away.

• Brom Bones played a trick on Ichabod and scared him away.

• _____

A TAKE A CLOSER LOOK

1 Theme Comparison: Mystery and Fantasy

Life is full of mysteries. There are many things we can't explain, especially when we are lonely or frightened. In the first story of Part Three, a lonely man believes that his missing wife will return by Saturday night. In the second story, a mysterious family next door has a strange fear of the rain. At the end of the last story, we wonder what really happened to Ichabod Crane.

With a partner, discuss the following questions.

1 If you could ask Mark Twain one question about Henry and his wife's disappearance, what would you ask?
2 Do you feel sorry for the Sakkaros? If you were the author, how would you end "Rain, Rain, Go Away?"
3 Which ending of "The Legend of Sleepy Hollow" do you think Washington Irving wants us to believe?

2 Freewriting

Write the word *mystery* at the top of a sheet of paper. Then write any words that come into your mind when you think of mystery. For 15 minutes, write about a mysterious event from a movie, a book, or your own life. What was the situation? Where did it take place? Who was in the event? Did the event frighten you? Was the mystery finally solved?

B REVIEW

1 Grammar Review

Circle the correct verb or verbs in parentheses to complete the following sentences.

1 I (go / am going / went / was going) to scary movies every Friday night.

2 Last Friday night, I (see / saw / am seeing / was seeing) a really scary movie.

3 My friends (come / was coming / are coming / came) with me.

4 While we (watched / watch / are watching / were watching) the movie, the lights (are turning / were turning / turned / turn) off.

5 Everyone in the theater (began / was beginning / is beginning / begins) to scream.

6 My friend Ichabod (drops / dropped / was dropping / is dropping) his popcorn while everyone (is screaming / screams / screamed / was screaming).

7 Right now, I (wrote / am writing / was writing / write) about last Friday night in my journal.

8 Now I (think / was thinking / thought / am thinking) that night wasn't scary – it was funny.

2 Vocabulary Review

The words in the list are in the word search box. Find the words in the box. The words are written across or down.

console	gloomy	loose	tension
cottage	human	manners	wailed
cozy	invite	novelty	wealthy
eventually	jealous	ominously	
forecast	letter	soldier	

```
U G F M A N N E R S Z D X M K C D M H U M
O L X M L D O I N V I T E M X U D C E Y R
M O S Z P W E A L T H Y V H W J Z T B F Z
I O O R E V E N T U A L L Y T E N S I O N
N M L J D J L E T T E R K Q G A B Q F R J
O Y D S W A I L E D C O N S O L E X R E B
U D I B M W E D J J W X B H Y O B Y I C T
S A E Q Y C O T T A G E R F H U M A N A J
L P R L G C O Z Y U K W S L X S R G M S L
Y X M M E G U M N L O O S E N O V E L T Y
```

C ELEMENTS OF A SHORT STORY

Filling Out the Elements Chart

This chart shows the five basic elements of a short story. You can find these elements on page 170. Some of the elements have been filled out for "Rain, Rain, Go Away." Complete the chart. Then copy the blank chart on page xvi and fill it out for "The Californian's Tale" or "The Legend of Sleepy Hollow" or for both stories. Share your charts with a partner or in a small group.

Elements of _____ *Rain, Rain, Go Away* _____
(name of story)

SETTING

CHARACTERS

PLOT

CONFLICT
The conflict is between the Sakkaros and their environment.

THEME(S)
A seemingly perfect family collapses under stress.

WEBQUEST

Find more information about the topics in Part Three by going on the Internet. Go to www.cambridge.org/discoveringfiction/wq and follow the instructions for doing a WebQuest. Have fun. Enjoy the quest!

PART FOUR

Close Relationships

FROM EARLY childhood, we all form close relationships with the people around us – our families, our classmates, our neighbors, our co-workers – and maybe we even fall in love. Some of these relationships make us very happy; others make us sad and disappointed. Through their characters, writers can help us understand relationships and how they make us feel.

In the first story you are about to read, a young man's images of race and culture destroy the happiness of the woman he loves. In the second story, a family keeps secrets from each other. In the final story, the relationship between a mother and her son is tested. As you read each story, think about how you would feel in the relationships if you were the main character.

CHAPTER 10

Its Wavering Image

EDITH EATON

A PREPARING TO READ

1 Think Before You Read

Answer the following questions:

1 Do you know anyone whose mother is from one race or culture and whose father is from another race or culture?
2 Do you think that a person from one race or culture should marry a person from another race or culture? Why or why not?
3 What advantages and disadvantages do you think that people of two races – biracial people – have? Explain your answer.

2 Picture Focus

With a partner, talk about the picture. Why do you think the young woman looks angry?

3 Words to Know

Study the following key words and expressions from the story. They all relate to race and culture. Then complete the paragraph using each word or expression once.

ethnicity racial, national, or cultural background	**foreign** of a country or custom that is not the same as yours
facial features eyes, nose, mouth, cheeks, and chin of a person	**customs** practices or habits of a person, group, or country
belong be a part of a place or group	**beliefs** ideas that a person or group believes are true

In today's world, it is not unusual to meet people who _____

to more than one race or one culture. When you meet them, it can be difficult

to know their _____ just by talking with them. They may

seem _____ to you even though they were born in the same

country as you. For example, the person may have the _____

_____ from more than one race. In addition, because the person

has grown up with parents from two different cultures, he or she may have an

unusual combination of _____ and _____.

4 Story Preview

Read the preview of the story. Then answer the questions in Making Predictions on the next page.

Pan is a half-white, half-Chinese girl. She lives with her Chinese father in Chinatown, in the Canadian city of Montreal. Her white mother is dead. Pan always feels comfortable with her father's people. She does not like to be with white people. That changes when Pan meets Mark Carson, a white journalist. They become friends, and then something happens between them.

5 Making Predictions

From the Story Preview, try to predict what will happen. Circle one choice below or write your own answer. Discuss your prediction with a partner.

What will happen as Pan and Mark become friends?

1 Pan will no longer be happy with Chinese people.

2 Pan and Mark will fall in love and get married.

3 Pan will decide she is not a white woman.

4 _____

6 Idioms and Expressions

You will find these idioms and expressions in the story:

sell one's soul do anything to get what one wants	**have no right** not be allowed to do something
shy away from avoid or stay away from something	**would rather** prefer
at home with comfortable with	**Don't you dare!** Never do that!

7 Literary Term: Conflict

Within a plot there is often a **conflict** or struggle. The conflict can be a fight or disagreement between characters, between characters and the environment, or inside a character's mind. Every story contains some type of conflict, and by the end of the story, the conflict ends.

Focus As you read the story, notice the conflict between the two main characters, Pan and Mark. What is their conflict? Also notice the conflict inside Pan's mind and how this conflict ends.

About the Author

Edith Eaton (1865–1914) was born to a Chinese mother and a British father. She grew up in a large family in Montreal, Quebec. While she was working as a typist, she began her career as a journalist. She wrote under the name Sui Sin Far. Her articles about the Chinese-Canadian community were published in several Montreal newspapers.

In the early 1900s, Eaton moved to the United States where she wrote about the Chinatowns in San Francisco, Seattle, and Boston. In 1912, she published her book of stories, *Mrs. Spring Fragrance.* "Its Wavering Image" is one of the stories.

Its Wavering Image

Pan was a half-white, half-Chinese girl. Her white mother was dead, so Pan lived alone with her Chinese father, Man Yu. Man Yu owned a small shop on Du Pont Street in Montreal's Chinatown. All her life Pan lived in Chinatown. She never thought about being different until she

5 met Mark Carson.

Mark Carson was a newspaper journalist. He was sent by his editor to write a story about life in Chinatown. He was a clever young man. He knew how to get people to tell him their secrets. In fact, people who knew him said he was "a man who would sell his soul for a story."

10 First, Mark went to the shop of Man Yu. Pan was in the shop. She was helping her father. She always shied away from white people. She was at home with her father's people. With her mother's, she felt strange.

When Mark first saw Pan, he wondered, "Is she Chinese, or white?" He wasn't sure of her ethnicity. Her facial features were unusual. His

15 editor told him, "She is an unusually smart girl. She can tell you more stories about the Chinese than any other person in the city." For this reason, Mark became Pan's friend. He was also attracted to her.

Mark was Pan's first white friend. She took him everywhere in Chinatown. He was welcomed in clubs where only Chinese were

20 allowed. Chinese groups invited him to their meetings. Everyone trusted him. Wherever he went with Pan, he was welcomed.

Soon, Pan and Mark fell in love. In the evenings, Pan took Mark up to her little apartment above her father's shop. They listened to a Chinese band playing music on the street below. Sometimes, her father would come up to ask if they wanted anything. Pan was proud of her father. She said, "I would rather have a Chinese for a father than a white one." Once, Mark asked, "Would you rather have a white man or a Chinese man for a husband?" For the first time, Pan did not have an answer.

One night, Mark took Pan's hand.

"Pan," he said, "you do not belong here. You are white!"

Pan cried out, "No, no."

"You are white," he repeated. "You have no right to be here."

"I was born here," she answered, "and the Chinese people see me as their own."

"But they do not understand you," he replied. "Your real self is foreign to them."

"They have an interest in me," Pan said. "Do not speak like that."

"But, I must. You have to decide what you will be – Chinese or white. You can't be both."

A little Chinese boy brought them tea and cakes. He was a cute child. Mark laughed and played with him. Pan smiled.

When they were alone again, they looked out the window to see the first quarter of the moon shining on the river. It was a beautiful night. With his hand on Pan's shoulder, Mark began to sing:

And forever, and forever
As long as the river flows.
The moon and its changing reflection
Is a symbol of love
And its wavering image here.

Listening to the song, Pan began to cry. She was so happy.

"Look at me," Mark said, "Oh, Pan. These tears show that you are white."

Pan lifted her wet face. "Kiss me, Pan," Mark said. It was their first kiss.

The next morning, Mark began work on the special news article, which he promised his editor. Two days later, the article entitled, "Its Wavering Image" appeared in the newspaper.

Pan's father threw the paper at his daughter's feet and left the room. Surprised at her father's anger, Pan picked up the paper and read the words. "Betrayed!" she cried. Mark's article had every Chinese secret she told him. He made fun of Chinese customs and beliefs. He made fun of her friends and family. She looked at the title, "Its Wavering Image."

Mark was back in the city after being away for two months. He was excited. This evening he would see Pan again. He was sure she forgot about the article he wrote. However, he was a little worried as he climbed the hill to her father's shop. Why didn't Pan answer his letters when he was away?

When she opened the door, she was not smiling. Mark tried to explain about his article in the newspaper.

"I knew they would not blame you, Pan," he said.

Pan said nothing.

"And I never used your name."

Still, she did not answer.

Pan looked different. She was not herself tonight. He usually saw her in American clothes. Tonight, she wore a Chinese dress.

"Pan," he asked, "Why are you wearing that dress?"

"Because I am a Chinese woman," she answered.

"You are not!" Mark said. "You are a white woman. Your kiss promised me that."

"A white woman!" Pan answered. "Don't you dare call me a white woman! I will never be a white woman. You are a white man – and what is a promise to a white man?"

After Mark left, a little girl and her mother came to Man Yu's shop. Pan was sitting on a chair. She had angry tears in her eyes. The little girl put her head next to Pan's.

"Look," said the mother, "how my little girl loves you. Maybe you will have a child some day, and all this sadness will pass away."

And Pan, being a Chinese woman, was comforted.

C UNDERSTANDING THE STORY

1 Reading Comprehension

With a partner or in a small group, discuss the following questions:

1 How does Pan meet Mark?
2 What does the newspaper editor tell Mark about Pan?
3 How does Pan help Mark learn about the people in Chinatown?
4 Why does Pan become angry with Mark?
5 At the end of the story, does Pan feel she is a white woman or a Chinese woman? Explain your answer.

2 Guessing Meaning from Context

The words in the list are in the story. Find the words in the story, and try to understand their meanings. Then answer the questions that follow the list. Use your own opinions, knowledge, or experiences.

journalist	welcomed	wavering	blame
editor	trusted	promised	comforted
clever	reflection	betrayed	
attracted	symbol	worried	

1 Do **editors** work only for newspapers?

No. Some editors work for books or magazines.

2 When you are sad, what makes you feel the most **comforted**?

3 If you were a **journalist**, what types of stories would you write?

4 Have you ever **promised** someone something that you could not give them? Explain.

5 Are you **worried** about anything right now? What are you worried about?

_____

6 What is a **symbol** of love?

_____

7 When you pass a shop window, do you ever look at your **reflection** in the window? Why or why not?

_____

8 What type of person are you most **attracted** to?

_____

9 Have any of your friends or family ever **betrayed** you? What did they do?

_____

10 What is a **clever** way to save money?

_____

11 Are you **wavering** on any decision right now? What decision are you wavering on?

_____

12 Where have you felt the most **welcomed** in your life?

_____

13 Who should you **blame** if you are unhappy?

_____

14 Who is your most **trusted** friend? Why is he or she the most **trusted**?

_____

3 Grammar: Simple Sentences

A simple sentence, or an independent clause, is a complete thought. It has <u>one</u> subject and <u>one</u> verb. In English, the subject comes before the verb. Other words can help complete the thought.

- A subject is a noun or pronoun. It is the person or thing that performs the action of a verb. Words like *it* or *there* can also be subjects.

  Examples:
  Man Yu owned a small shop in Chinatown.
  The small shop was always busy.
  It sold food and other items.
  There were many people in the shop.

- A verb tells what the subject is or what the subject does.

  Examples:
  Pan **was** a half-white, half-Chinese girl.
  She **lived** in Chinatown.

- Other words can come before the subject or after the verb to complete the thought.

  Examples:
  Mark Carson was **a newspaper journalist**.
  Every day he wrote **news articles**.
  He wrote **an article about the people of Chinatown**.

- If a sentence has more than one clause, that is, it has more than one subject and one verb, it is a complex sentence (see page 150 for more on complex sentences).

  Examples:
  Mark was excited. (simple sentence)
  Mark was going to see Pan again. (simple sentence)
  Mark was excited because he was going to see Pan again.
     (complex sentence)

Application 1   In the story, the author writes many short simple sentences. In the third paragraph, every sentence is a simple sentence. Read the paragraph again, and underline the subject and circle the verb in each sentence. Put *S* above the subject and *V* above the verb.

First, Mark went to the shop of Man Yu. Pan was in the shop. She was helping her father. She always shied away from white people. She was at home with her father's people. With her mother's, she felt strange.

Application 2   The following sentences all come from the story. Some are simple sentences and some are complex sentences. Mark the simple sentences *SS* and the complex sentences *CX*.

_CX_   1   She never thought about being different until she met Mark Carson.

____   2   Mark Carson was a newspaper journalist.

____   3   Wherever he went with Pan, he was welcomed.

____   4   For the first time, Pan did not have an answer.

____   5   A little Chinese boy brought them tea and cakes.

____   6   With his hand on Pan's shoulder, Mark began to sing.

____   7   He made fun of Chinese customs and beliefs.

____   8   When she opened the door, she was not smiling.

____   9   Tonight she wore a Chinese dress.

____   10   After Mark left, a little girl and her mother came to Man Yu's shop.

D THINKING CRITICALLY

1 Discussing the Story

With a partner or in a small group, discuss the following questions:

1 Why do you think Mark is attracted to Pan?
2 Why does Pan feel that Mark betrayed her?
3 What do you think Mark wants to happen when he comes back to see Pan?
4 Why does Mark want Pan to be white?
5 Why is the story titled "Its Wavering Image"? What are the wavering images in the story?

2 Making Inferences

Authors often write something that can have more than one meaning. You need to figure out what the author means. This is called making inferences. Read the following sentences from the story. Then circle the answer that shows the author's meaning. If you need help, look back at the story. Discuss your answers.

1 . . . he was "a man who would sell his soul for a story."
   a Mark loved to write stories.
   b Mark would do anything he could to get a story.
   c Mark didn't have a soul.

2 "Pan," he said, "You do not belong here. You are white!"
   a Mark thinks that Man Yu isn't really Pan's father.
   b Mark thinks the people of Chinatown do not like Pan.
   c Mark thinks that Pan is more white than Chinese in her behavior.

3 Pan's father threw the paper at his daughter's feet and left the room.
   a Pan's father didn't have time to read the paper.
   b Pan's father was very angry about something in the paper.
   c Pan's father finished reading the newspaper and had to leave quickly.

4 He usually saw her in American clothes. Tonight she wore a Chinese dress.
   a Mark expected Pan to look and behave like a white woman.
   b Mark thought Pan looked beautiful in her Chinese dress.
   c Mark forgot what Pan looked like.

3 Analyzing the Story: Conflict

As you read on page 132, conflict can happen between people or inside the mind of one person. In this story, Pan's image of herself begins to waver when she meets Mark. The following diagram shows Pan's thoughts about her image from the beginning of the story to the end. Find the lines from the story for each thought. Write the line numbers in the blanks to complete the chart.

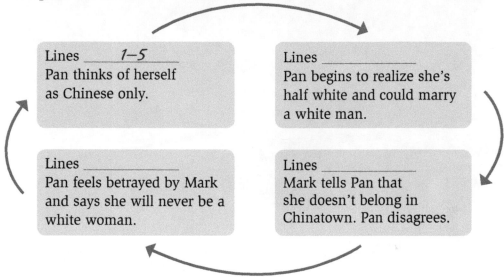

Lines ___*1–5*___
Pan thinks of herself as Chinese only.

Lines _____
Pan begins to realize she's half white and could marry a white man.

Lines _____
Pan feels betrayed by Mark and says she will never be a white woman.

Lines _____
Mark tells Pan that she doesn't belong in Chinatown. Pan disagrees.

4 Summarizing

Put the following sentences in the correct order to summarize the story. Write the numbers from 1 to 6 to show the order. The first one has been done for you.

____ Mark's story makes fun of Chinese people and their culture.

____ Mark and Pan fall in love.

_1_ Mark Carson wants to write an article about Chinatown.

____ Mark meets Pan and wonders if she is Chinese or white.

____ Pan feels betrayed by Mark and chooses to be Chinese, not white.

____ Pan introduces Mark to her Chinese friends and takes him everywhere in Chinatown.

5 Writing

Pretend to be Mark. Write your thoughts as you walk home from your last visit with Pan.

CHAPTER 11

The Tree of Knowledge

Henry James

A PREPARING TO READ

1 Think Before You Read

Answer the following questions:

1 What does it mean to "keep a secret"?
2 Is it easy or difficult for you to keep a secret? Explain your answer.
3 What kind of secret should you keep? What kind of secret should you tell?

2 Picture Focus

With a partner, talk about the picture. What is the relationship between the two men?

3 Words to Know

Study the following key words from the story. They all relate to the career of an artist. Then complete the paragraph using each word once.

sculptor artist who shapes art pieces out of wood, stone, metal, etc.	**famous** well known by many people
sculptures pieces of art made out of wood, stone, metal, etc.	**create** make new and original ideas and things
painters artists who use oil, watercolors, or other types of paint to make pictures	**talent** special ability to do or make something
	master person who has great ability and experience to do something

The career of an artist is not easy. Artists must have both passion and

_____ for making art. They must be able to _____

art that other people will like. Some artists are _____ and use oil

or watercolors to make beautiful pictures. Other artists use wood, stone, or

metal to make interesting _____. This type of artist is called a

_____. To make money as an artist, artists must become

_____. If many people see their artwork and like it, they may

buy it. And people will pay more money for the art of a _____.

4 Story Preview

Read the preview of the story. Then answer the question in Making Predictions on the next page.

Peter Brench is a single man. He is a very close friend to Mr. and Mrs. Mallow and their son Lance. Mr. Mallow is a sculptor. Lance wants to be an artist like his father. Mrs. Mallow also wants her son to be an artist, but Peter tries to discourage Lance. He thinks Lance should stay at Cambridge University to become a lawyer or banker. However, Lance decides to go to Paris to study art.

5 Making Predictions

From the Story Preview, try to predict what will happen. Circle one choice below or write your own answer. Discuss your prediction with a partner.

What will happen to Lance after he goes to Paris?

1 He will become a famous artist.

2 He will miss his family and come home.

3 He will learn something about his father, his mother, and Peter.

4 _____

6 Idioms and Expressions

You will find these idioms and expressions in the story:

follow in someone's footsteps choose the same career as your father, mother, or other person **reason with** try to change someone's opinion	**I see.** I understand. **world revolves around someone** all attention goes to one person **come to light** become known **deal openly** speak the truth

7 Literary Term: Irony

Irony is when something happens that is different from what the readers or characters in a story understand or expect to happen. In this story, the author uses family secrets to create some irony.

Focus   As you read the story, think about the characters and the secrets they keep from each other. Think about the characters' expectations. What truth do they learn by the end of the story? Do all the characters learn the truth?

About the Author

Henry James (1843–1916) was born in New York City. His parents were wealthy and encouraged their children to get a good education. James started studying at Harvard Law School in 1862. However, he became more interested in writing book reviews and stories and gave up his law studies.

James traveled to Europe several times as a child. As an adult, he briefly tried living and writing in Paris, and later he moved permanently to London. As an American living in Europe, James wrote about the conflict between American and European manners and customs. This theme occurs in many of his novels and short stories. Some of his most famous novels are *The American*, *The Bostonians*, *Washington Square*, and *Daisy Miller*.

The Tree of Knowledge

Peter Brench was a close friend of Mr. and Mrs. Mallow. The Mallows were married for many years, but Peter was still unmarried at the age of fifty. Peter was in love with Mrs. Mallow, yet he never told her. In fact, he never married because of his love for her. Instead, he spent
5 almost every day with the couple. They ate dinners together and traveled together.

Mr. Mallow was a sculptor. He was able to have a career as an artist because Mrs. Mallow was wealthy. Peter liked Mr. Mallow, but he thought his sculptures were terrible.
10 Peter never told his friends the truth. He never showed his dislike for Mr. Mallow's art or his love for Mrs. Mallow. Thus, Peter was the perfect friend.

The Mallows had a son named Lance. They asked Peter to be his godfather. Peter agreed, and he loved his godson.
15 Lance grew up thinking he would be an artist like his father, and Mrs. Mallow encouraged Lance to follow in his father's footsteps. Lance loved painting, so he wanted to become a painter.

Mrs. Mallow felt Lance had inherited his father's passion, and he might even be a famous artist someday. On the other hand, Peter discouraged painting as a career for his godson. He wanted Lance to study for a career in law or banking at Cambridge University. Peter studied at Cambridge University when he was young. As a result, he asked the university to accept Lance, and the university agreed.

"I was hoping he would lose interest in painting. Being an artist isn't a good career for him."

"But why not, Peter? Why shouldn't he create art?" asked Mrs. Mallow. "Look at the joy his father has in making his sculptures."

"Do you think he'll be like his father?" asked Peter.

"Lance has passion. Some people may criticize his art one day, yet his passion will be stronger than the criticism. He'll find happiness in his work."

Eventually, Peter stopped trying to reason with Mrs. Mallow because Lance had now become a student at Cambridge University.

Soon, however, it was clear that Lance wasn't a very good student. He still thought about painting, and he decided to leave the university and go to Paris to become an artist.

Lance asked Peter, "Do you think I have talent?"

Peter put his arm around Lance and said, "How do I know?"

"Are you saying you can't judge my talent?" Lance continued.

"No, I think that becoming an artist would not be a good life for you. Furthermore, if you decide to give up Paris and stay at Cambridge, I will pay all of your tuition."

"Don't you want me to go to Paris?"

"I think Paris will be wrong for you."

"But why do you want me to stay at home?"

"The four of us are so good together. We are safe together. Let's not spoil it."

"Then what career will I have?"

"I'll take care of you."

"Do you think there's something wrong with me? Do you think I can't become a success?"

"Well, what is a success?"

"I guess people who do what they want to do like my father does. He is happy; therefore, he is successful."

Finally, Lance left Cambridge and went to Paris. He studied art seriously. Occasionally, he came home to visit. A year later, on one of his visits, he had a long talk with Peter about his experience.

"Peter, now I know why you didn't want me to go to Paris to study art. Something terrible has happened to me."

"What is it, my boy? I see from your face that you're not very happy."

The enthusiasm Lance had before going to Paris was gone.

"I'm a terrible artist, Peter. I realize that now. It's a big disappointment to me. I thought the artist's life would be mine. Now, I have nothing. Do you know what I found out in Paris? I learned what I cannot do. In addition, I compared my father's sculptures with other sculptures I saw, and I could see that my father is not a good artist at all. Is that why you didn't want me to go to Paris?"

Peter stared at him. Peter had never discussed Mallow's sculptures with Lance. He thought that Lance, like his mother, believed Mallow was a talented artist. Now Peter understood that Lance knew the truth.

> Peter had never discussed Mallow's sculptures with Lance. He thought that Lance, like his mother, believed Mallow was a talented artist. Now Peter understood that Lance knew the truth.

Lance looked at Peter and said, "Do you think I didn't know about my father's lack of talent? Even before I went to Paris and saw great art, I knew my father was not very good. My parents want people to believe my father is a master; however, for a long time, I've known that my father is not good enough to be a master. My father is a dreamer, and my mother feeds his dreams."

Peter said, "Why didn't you tell me this before?"

Lance answered, "Why did *you* keep your knowledge a secret from *me* for so many years?"

"I did it for your mother."

"Oh, I see."

"Now Lance, you must promise to never say a word to your mother."

"Are you sure my mother doesn't know?"

"If she does, she's too wonderful."

"You think my mother is wonderful? Have you always loved her?"

Peter didn't say anything for a minute. Then, he lowered his head. "I've loved you all. You're my family."

Lance continued, "Poor, Peter. It must be so hard for you. You've had to keep so many secrets. Now, you have my secrets as well – that I know the truth about my father's lack of talent, and that I am a failure as an artist. My father would be angry if he knew the truth about my failure. I will go back to Paris and try painting again. Maybe this time I will be successful."

Six months later, Lance returned home again. This time, his father wanted to see the work Lance created. Mallow did not expect his son to be a master as he was; nevertheless, he expected Lance to have something to show for all the time he spent in Paris.

After Lance showed his work to his father, he went to see Peter. There were tears in Lance's eyes.

"I don't know how you do it, Peter. How do you pretend my father's work is good? I had to show my father all my work. At the same time, I had to pretend that his work is better than mine and that he is a master. Doesn't it make you sad to pretend all the time? I know you love my mother, but she only cares about my father. She loves us, but her world revolves around him."

Peter smiled sadly, "That's how it should be. I don't tell her the truth because I know how much she cares about him. I protect her; therefore, you must protect her as well."

"Dear Peter, I think it's time for you to know. My mother does know the truth. She came to my room yesterday and spent an hour talking to me. She does know about my father. She has always known. All these years she has been pretending, too. She has pretended he was a great artist to protect him.

"All these secrets we kept from each other have finally come to light. Now we are free and perhaps, we can deal openly with each other. Knowledge may be dangerous, but it can also bring us closer. So you see, Peter, your original reason to keep me away from Paris was to keep me from gaining knowledge. You didn't want me to know the truth about my father or about my mother. But I do know."

After that, Lance left the room with a smile on his face and a new joy in his soul. He was now a man, and Peter was proud of him.

Peter remained silent. He thought to himself, "Maybe my original reason to keep Lance away from Paris was to keep myself from gaining knowledge. Maybe I never wanted to know the truth."

C UNDERSTANDING THE STORY

1 Reading Comprehension

With a partner or in a small group, discuss the following questions:

1 Why does Peter Brench spend so much time with the Mallows?
2 Why does Mrs. Mallow want Lance to become an artist?
3 Why doesn't Peter want Lance to become an artist?
4 What does Lance learn in Paris?
5 What secret has Mrs. Mallow kept for many years?

2 Guessing Meaning from Context

The words on the left are in the story. Find them in the story and try to understand their meanings. Match each word to the correct definition on the right. Write the letter of the definition on the blank line.

_f_ 1 terrible

____ 2 encourage

____ 3 discourage

____ 4 joy

____ 5 criticize

____ 6 judge

____ 7 tuition

____ 8 success

____ 9 enthusiasm

____ 10 compare

____ 11 truth

____ 12 wonderful

____ 13 failure

____ 14 protect

a doing well at something; reaching a goal

b very good

c find bad things about someone or something

d money for a college education

e look for the good or bad in something and give an opinion about it

f very bad

g give someone hope; tell someone to keep trying to do something

h prevent someone or something from being hurt

i not doing well at something; not reaching a goal

j great interest or energy about something

k great happiness

l not give someone hope; tell someone to stop trying to do something

m consider how one thing is similar or equal to another thing

n fact

3 Grammar: Connecting Sentences

Writers sometimes connect a simple sentence (a sentence with one independent clause – see page 138) to another simple sentence to make a complex sentence. When writers connect two sentences, they show a relationship between them. Two ways to connect sentences are to use conjunctions or transitions.

● The seven basic conjunctions are *and, but, so, or, nor, for,* and *yet.* Use a comma (,) before the conjunction when it joins two independent clauses.

Examples:
Peter was in love with Mrs. Mallow, **but** he never told her.
(complete thought with a subject and verb + another complete thought with a subject and verb)
Lance returned home, **and** his father wanted to see the work he created.

● Some common transition words are listed below. Use a comma (,) after the transition word. Note that a semicolon (;) or a period (.) must come before the transition word.

1 To add more information, use words like *in fact, in addition, furthermore, for example, also.*
2 To show a contrast, use words like *instead, however, nevertheless, on the other hand.*
3 To show a result, use words like *therefore, as a result, thus.*
4 To show time, use words like *eventually, occasionally, first, second, then, later, now, finally, at the same time.*

Examples:
Mrs. Mallow encouraged Lance to be an artist. **However,** Peter discouraged this career for his godson.
(*However* shows a contrast between Mrs. Mallow's idea and Peter's idea.)
Peter liked Mr. Mallow; **therefore,** he couldn't tell him that he didn't like his sculptures.
(*Therefore* shows the result of Peter's friendship – he can't tell his friend the truth.)

Application 1   The following sentences and clauses are from the story. Without looking back at the story, choose the correct words to connect them.

1 Peter was in love with Mrs. Mallow, _____*yet*_____ (and/yet/so) he never told her. _____*In fact,*_____ (Nevertheless,/Finally,/In fact,) he never married because of his love for her.

2 Mr. Mallow was a sculptor. . . . Peter liked Mr. Mallow, _____ (so/and/but) he thought his sculptures were terrible.

3 "Lance has passion. Some people may criticize his art one day, _____ (so/yet/or) his passion will be stronger than the criticism."

4 Finally, Lance left Cambridge and went to Paris. . . . _____ (In addition,/Occasionally,/As a result,) he came home to visit.

5 "In addition, I compared my father's sculptures with other sculptures I saw, _____ (but/so/and) I could see that my father is not a good artist at all."

Application 2   Connect the following sentences. Use conjunctions or transitions. Use the comma, semicolon, or period correctly.

1 Peter is 50 years old. He has never been married.

   Peter is 50 years old, but he has never been married.

2 Peter spends a lot of time with the Mallows. He is not a member of the family.

   _____

3 Peter loves Lance. He wants to protect him from the truth.

   _____

4 Lance finds the truth in Paris. His mother tells him her secret about his father.

   _____

D THINKING CRITICALLY

1 Discussing the Story

With a partner or in a small group, discuss the following questions:

1 What are Peter's secrets about the Mallows? Why doesn't he tell anyone his secrets?
2 Do you think Mr. and Mrs. Mallow have a good relationship? Why or why not?
3 How does Lance change after he goes to Paris?
4 What do you think Lance means when he tells Peter that knowledge can be dangerous, but it can also bring people closer together?
5 Which character in the story do you like best? Why do you like that character?

2 Making Inferences

Authors often write something that can have more than one meaning. You need to figure out what the author means. This is called making inferences. Read the following sentences from the story. Then circle the answer that shows the author's meaning. If you need help, look back at the story. Discuss your answers.

1 "Do you think he'll be like his father?" asked Peter.
   a Peter thinks that Lance will become a sculptor.
   b Peter thinks that Lance should be a banker.
   c Peter is worried that Lance will have no talent because his father has no talent.

2 "The four of us are so good together. We are safe together. Let's not spoil it."
   a Peter does not want Lance to go to Paris because Paris is dangerous.
   b Peter does not want Lance to go to Paris because Lance and the Mallows are like a close family.
   c Peter will be angry with Lance if Lance goes to Paris.

3 "My father is a dreamer, and my mother feeds his dreams."
   a Lance feels that his mother will do anything to encourage her husband.
   b Lance thinks that his mother gives his father lots of money.
   c Lance thinks that his mother cooks delicious meals for her husband.

3 Analyzing the Story: Irony

As you read on page 144, irony can be how readers or characters see or understand the truth. On the left side of the chart are secrets or beliefs. On the right side of the chart are the ironies of the secrets or beliefs. Fill in the blank lines to complete each sentence.

THE SECRETS AND BELIEFS	THE IRONY
Peter Brench loves Mrs. Mallow and thinks it is a secret.	However, _everyone knows_ that Peter loves her.
Peter Brench doesn't want Lance to know that his father is a terrible artist.	Nevertheless, Lance _____ that his father is not a good artist.
Mr. Mallow thinks that he, himself, is a good artist.	On the other hand, everyone else thinks _____ .
Peter Brench thinks he is protecting Mrs. Mallow by not telling her that her husband's art is terrible.	However, Mrs. Mallow doesn't need Peter's protection because she _____ .

4 Summarizing

Put the following sentences in the correct order to summarize the story. Write the numbers 1 to 6 to show the order. The first one has been done for you.

____ Lance realizes he's not a good artist.

____ Lance gains knowledge about himself and his family's secrets.

_1_ Peter Brench is a close friend of the Mallow family.

____ Lance wants to be an artist like his father.

____ Peter becomes the godfather to the Mallows' son Lance.

____ Peter doesn't want Lance to study art in Paris.

5 Writing

Continue the story. Pretend it is five years later. What has happened to Mr. and Mrs. Mallow, Lance, and Peter? Describe their relationships with each other.

CHAPTER 12

All the Years of Her Life

MORLEY CALLAGHAN

A PREPARING TO READ

1 Think Before You Read

Answer the following questions:

1 Why do you think some people steal – take things from other people or places without paying for them?
2 What should employers do if one of their employees steals things from them?
3 What should parents do when their children steal?

2 Picture Focus

With a partner, talk about the picture. Who are the three people? What are the man and woman talking about?

3 Words to Know

Study the following key words and expressions from the story. They all relate to *stealing*. Then complete the paragraph using each word or expression once.

nervous worried or frightened	**jail** a place that the police use for people who have been arrested
thief a person who steals something	
robs steals something from someone or some place	**caught red-handed** when someone is found doing something wrong
arrest when the police take a person and put him or her in jail	

There are many different types of stealing. Some people take small things from family or friends. Other people steal from their employers or shoplift from stores. A _____ is a person who usually makes a career out of stealing. He or she often _____ houses or banks and does not get _____ easily. This type of person keeps stealing until he or she is _____ _____. If this happens, and the police come to the scene, the police will _____ this person and put him or her in _____.

4 Story Preview

Read the preview of the story. Then answer the questions in Making Predictions on the next page.

Alfred, a teenage boy who has left school, gets into trouble when he is caught stealing from his employer, Mr. Carr. His mother comes to help him as she has done many times before. But this time, Alfred is surprised by how calm she is. When they walk home, Alfred's mother is quiet and doesn't speak to him. She acts as if he isn't walking next to her.

5 Making Predictions

From the Story Preview, try to predict what will happen. Circle one choice below or write your own answer. Discuss your prediction with a partner.

What will Alfred's mother do when they get home?

1 She will tell Alfred to leave home.

2 She will never speak to Alfred again.

3 She will tell Alfred's father about the stealing.

4 _____

6 Idioms and Expressions

You will find these idioms and expressions in the story:

just a moment a short time; people say this or "just a minute" when they want someone to wait	**hang around with** spend a lot of time with someone
catch your breath return to normal breathing after excitement or activity	**fire someone** when an employer tells someone to leave a job because the person did something bad
get in trouble do something wrong	**Thank goodness!** people say this when they are happy that something good happened that they expected to be bad
hold a job have a job; keep working at a job	

7 Literary Term: Tone

Tone shows the writer's feelings about the subject and characters of the story. The tone may be happy or sad, calm or angry, funny or serious. Through description and dialogue, the writer sets, or creates, the tone.

Focus As you read the story, think about the tone of the story. Is there more than one tone? Notice the descriptions and dialogues that help set the tone of the story. Notice if the tone changes during the story.

About the Author

Morley Edward Callaghan (1903–1990) was born and raised in Toronto, Ontario. He attended the University of Toronto Law School, but he never practiced law. Instead, he became a newspaper reporter for the Toronto Daily Star. Callaghan became friends with the famous American author Ernest Hemingway, who was working in Canada at the time as a reporter. It was Hemingway who encouraged Callaghan to write short stories.

After Callaghan married, he and his wife went to Paris. They spent several months in Paris and were part of a group of writers that included Hemingway, James Joyce, and F. Scott Fitzgerald. During this time in Paris, Hemingway challenged Callaghan to a fighting match. Callaghan, who had been a fighter in college, knocked Hemingway to the ground, and Hemingway never forgave him.

Callaghan wrote short stories, short novels, and nonfiction. He became a well-known writer in Canada and the United States. One of his two sons, Barry Callaghan, also became a writer and poet. He wrote about his father in *Barrelhouse Kings* (1998).

All the Years of Her Life

Alfred Higgins worked in a drugstore. One night, as he was getting ready to leave for the day, he took off his white jacket and put on his coat. Sam Carr, who owned the drugstore, was standing near the cash register.[1] Most nights, he didn't look at Alfred and just said, "Good
5   night." Tonight, he said softly, "Just a moment, Alfred. Just a moment before you go."

Alfred started to button his coat and felt nervous. His heart began to beat so loud it was hard for him to catch his breath. "What is it, Mr. Carr?"

"Maybe you should take a few things out of your pocket before you
10 go," said Mr. Carr.

---

[1]**cash register**: a machine used in stores for keeping money from a sale or giving money as change

"What things? What are you talking about?"

"You have a compact[2] and a lipstick and two tubes of toothpaste in your pocket, Alfred."

"What do you mean? Are you calling me a thief?" Alfred's face got red, and he knew he looked insulted. Sam Carr's blue eyes were shining behind his glasses, and his lips were moving underneath his gray mustache. He nodded his head a few times, and Alfred became frightened. Slowly he put his hand in the deep pocket of his coat. He never looked at Sam Carr's eyes as he took out a compact, a lipstick, and two tubes of toothpaste. He put them one by one on the counter.

"How long have you been stealing from me?" asked Mr. Carr.

"This is the first time I took anything, Mr. Carr."

> "How long have you been stealing from me?"

"Do you expect me to believe that? You've probably been robbing the store for a while. I liked you, Alfred. I trusted you, and now, I'll have to call a policeman. You're a fool, and maybe I should call your father and tell him you're a fool. Maybe I should let him know I'm going to have you arrested and put in jail."

"My father's not at home. He's a printer, and he works nights," said Alfred.

"Who's at home?"

"My mother, I guess."

"Then we'll see what she says," and he went to the telephone and dialed her number.

"Just a minute. Do you have to tell her?"

He wanted to sound like a big guy who could take care of himself, but there was still a childish hope that someone at home would come and help him.

Alfred left school and lived at home with his parents. His older brothers were married and his sister just got married, so it was finally easier for his parents. But Alfred always got in trouble and couldn't hold a job for very long.

"Yes, that's right, Mrs. Higgins. Your boy's in trouble, I'm afraid. You better come here in a hurry." Alfred heard Mr. Carr speaking to his mother.

Alfred knew his mother would come rushing in. Maybe she would be crying, and she would push him away when he tried to talk to her. Yet he hoped she would arrive before Mr. Carr saw the policeman who usually walked by the store.

While they waited, they didn't speak. Then they heard someone

---

[2]**compact**: a small box for women's face powder

tapping on the glass door. Mr. Carr opened the door and said, "Come in, Mrs. Higgins." He looked angry.

55 Mrs. Higgins looked as if she was going to bed when she got the phone call. Her hair was tied and covered with a hat. Her coat was wrapped around her tightly. She was large and round and had a friendly smile on her face. Most of the store lights were turned off, and at first, she didn't see Alfred. He was standing in the dark at the end of the counter. When

60 she saw him, she looked at him with her blue eyes and smiled. She was calm and dignified. She gave Mr. Carr her hand and said, "I'm Mrs. Higgins. I'm Alfred's mother. Is he in trouble?"

Mr. Carr was a little surprised by her lack of fear. "He is. He's been stealing from the store. I caught him red-handed. He took little things

65 like compacts, toothpaste, and lipstick. It's stuff he can sell easily."

"Is it true, Alfred?"

"Yes."

"Why have you been doing it?"

"I wanted to have more money, I guess."

70 "For what?"

"When I hang around with the guys, I guess."

Mrs. Higgins touched Mr. Carr's arm gently and spoke as though she didn't want to disturb him. She was serious and shy as she asked, "What did you plan to do, Mr. Carr?"

75 "I was going to call a policeman. That's what I should do."

"Yes, maybe. I can't tell you what to do because he's my son. Yet sometimes I think a little good advice is the best thing for a boy when he's at a certain period of his life."

Alfred was amazed at his mother's quiet behavior. If they were at

80 home and someone said Alfred was going to be arrested, she would be crying. Yet here she was standing there with a gentle smile on her face saying, "Maybe it would be better to just let him come home with me. He looks like a big fellow, doesn't he? It takes some of them a long time to get any sense."

85 Both adults looked at Alfred. Alfred felt uncomfortable. He knew Mr. Carr realized that his mother was really a fine woman. There was only the sound of his mother's soft, confident voice in the store. Without being excited or frightened, Mrs. Higgins showed dignity in the dark store.

90 Mr. Carr nodded his head. "Of course, I want to help him learn to do what is right. I tell you what I'll do. I'll just fire him and I won't tell the police. Okay?" Then he shook hands with Mrs. Higgins.

"I'll never forget your kindness, Mr. Carr," she said.

"Sorry we had to meet this way."

95 They acted as if they liked each other, as if they had known each other a long time. "Good night, sir."

"Good night, Mrs. Higgins. I'm truly sorry."

The mother and son walked along the street together. Mrs. Higgins took long steps, and her serious face looked worried. Alfred was afraid to speak to her. He was afraid of the silence between them. The longer they walked in silence, the more he realized how strong his mother was. He wondered what she was thinking. She seemed to forget that he was walking beside her. Finally, he said, "Thank goodness it turned out like that. I certainly won't get in trouble like that again."

"Be quiet. Don't speak to me. You've disgraced me again and again," she said angrily.

"That's the last time. That's all I'm saying, Mom."

When they arrived home and his mother took off her coat, Alfred saw that she had put on a dress quickly before she went to the store. "You're a bad one. You are always in trouble. Why do you stand there? Go to bed. I'm going to make a cup of tea. Remember now, don't say anything about tonight to your father."

Alfred went upstairs and got undressed. He heard his mother in the kitchen filling the tea kettle, putting it on the stove, and moving a chair. He could remember Mr. Carr listening to her talk simply. Alfred felt a pride in her strength and calmness when she spoke to Mr. Carr. "I'd like to tell her she was great with Mr. Carr."

Alfred went downstairs to the kitchen. He watched his mother pour a cup of tea. He watched silently as his mother sat there. Her face was frightened and not like the face of the woman who was so confident before in the drugstore.

When she reached for the kettle, her hand was trembling and she spilled some water on the stove. Leaning back in the chair, she sighed and lifted the cup to her lips. She swallowed the hot tea. Then she sat up straight, though her hand still trembled. She looked very old.

Alfred realized that his mother always trembled whenever he was in trouble. This trembling had been inside her when she rushed to the drugstore. He watched his mother, and he didn't speak, but at that moment, his youth seemed to be over. All the years of her life showed in her trembling hand as she raised the cup to her lips. This seemed to be the first time he ever really looked at his mother.

C UNDERSTANDING THE STORY

1 Reading Comprehension

With a partner or in a small group, discuss the following questions:

1 How does Alfred act when Mr. Carr asks him to take things out of his pocket?
2 How does Alfred expect his mother to act when she comes to the drugstore?
3 What does Mrs. Higgins say to Mr. Carr? Is Alfred surprised?
4 How does Mrs. Higgins behave when she and Alfred walk home?
5 What does Alfred notice about his mother when she is drinking her tea?

2 Guessing Meaning from Context

The words in the list and the sentences that follow are in the story. Read the sentences and circle the letter of the best meaning of the **bold** word in each sentence.

insulted	calm	stuff	confident	trembling
tapping	dignified	disturb	kindness	sighed
wrapped	surprised	sense	disgraced	swallowed

1 Alfred's face got red, and he knew he looked **insulted**.
   a like he had a fever
   b unhappy with what Mr. Carr said
   c afraid of Mr. Carr

2 Then they heard someone **tapping** on the glass door.
   a dancing
   b writing
   c knocking

3 Her coat was **wrapped** around her tightly.
   a papered
   b covered
   c open

4 She was **calm** and dignified.
   a excited
   b nervous
   c relaxed

5 She was calm and **dignified**.
   a respectable
   b lonely
   c charming

6 Mr. Carr was a little **surprised** by her lack of fear.
  a amazed   **c** excited
  b happy

7 "It's **stuff** he can sell easily."
  a food   **c** old items
  b things

8 Mrs. Higgins touched Mr. Carr's arm gently and spoke as though she didn't want to **disturb** him.
  a annoy   **c** insult
  b see

9 "It takes some of them a long time to get any **sense**."
  a money   **c** touch
  b good judgment

10 There was only the sound of his mother's soft, **confident** voice in the store.
  a positive and clear   **c** clever and encouraging
  b quiet and scared

11 "I'll never forget your **kindness**, Mr. Carr," she said.
  a family   **c** goodness
  b bravery

12 "You've **disgraced** me again and again," she said angrily.
  a made other people hate   **c** made other people
  b made other people lose   uncomfortable with
     respect for

13 When she reached for the kettle, her hand was **trembling**, and she spilled some water on the stove.
  a shaking   **c** not moving
  b very hot

14 Leaning back in the chair, she **sighed** and lifted the cup to her lips.
  a spoke as she breathed out   **c** smiled as she breathed out
  b made a soft noise as she
     breathed out

15 She **swallowed** the hot tea.
  a spilled   **c** drank
  b boiled

3 Grammar: Forming Questions

Two types of questions in English are *Yes/No* questions and *Wh-* questions.

- *Yes/No* questions can be answered with *yes* or *no*.

  To turn a simple present or simple past statement into a *Yes/No* question, use *do, does,* or *did* + the subject + the main form of the verb.

  Examples:
  Statement: *Alfred has two tubes of toothpaste in his pocket.*
  Question: *<u>Does</u> Alfred <u>have</u> two tubes of toothpaste in his pocket?*
  Statement: *Alfred stole the toothpaste from Mr. Carr.*
  Question: *<u>Did</u> Alfred <u>steal</u> the toothpaste from Mr. Carr?*

  To turn a present continuous or past continuous statement into a *Yes/No* question, change the order of the subject and the *be* verb.

  Examples:
  Statement: *<u>Mrs. Higgins</u> <u>is</u> talking to Mr. Carr.*
  Question: *<u>Is</u> <u>Mrs. Higgins</u> talking to Mr. Carr?*
  Statement: *<u>Alfred and his mother</u> <u>were</u> walking silently.*
  Question: *<u>Were</u> <u>Alfred and his mother</u> walking silently?*

- *Wh-* questions ask for information. They begin with words like *who, what, when, where, why,* and *how.*

  Examples:
  Statement: *Alfred has two tubes of toothpaste in his pocket.*
  Question: *<u>Why</u> <u>does</u> Alfred <u>have</u> two tubes of toothpaste in his pocket?*
  Statement: *Alfred stole the toothpaste from Mr. Carr.*
  Question: *<u>What</u> <u>did</u> Alfred <u>steal</u> from Mr. Carr?*

  To turn a present continuous or past continuous statement into a *Wh-* question, add a *Wh-* question word and change the order of the subject and the *be* verb.

  Example:
  Statement: *<u>Mrs. Higgins</u> is talking to Mr. Carr.*
  Question: *<u>Why</u> <u>is</u> <u>Mrs. Higgins</u> talking to Mr. Carr?*

Application 1 Correct the following questions from the story. Some questions are missing words. Some use the wrong verb form. Some use the wrong word order. Then capitalize the first letter of the question, and put a question mark at the end.

1 what you talking about

What are you talking about?

2 are calling me a thief

_____

3 you expect me to believe that

_____

4 do you has to tell her

_____

5 he is in trouble

_____

6 what you does plan to do, Mr. Carr

_____

Application 2 Now write two questions to ask Alfred, Mr. Carr, or Mrs. Higgins something about their feelings or actions. Use *Yes/No* or *Wh-* questions.

1 Alfred, _____?

2 Alfred, _____?

3 Mr. Carr, _____?

4 Mr. Carr, _____?

5 Mrs. Higgins, _____?

6 Mrs. Higgins, _____?

D THINKING CRITICALLY

1 Discussing the Story

With a partner or in a small group, discuss the following questions:

1 Why do you think Alfred doesn't want Mr. Carr to call his mother?
2 Do you think Alfred will steal again? Why or why not?
3 Do you think Mr. Carr should have fired Alfred, called the police, or told his father? Explain your answer.
4 What does Alfred understand about his mother and her life when he sees her hand trembling?

2 Making Inferences

Authors often write something that can have more than one meaning. You need to figure out what the author means. This is called making inferences. Read the following quotes from the story. Then circle the answer that shows the author's meaning. If you need help, look back at the story. Discuss your answers.

1 Alfred says to Mr. Carr, "What do you mean? Are you calling me a thief?"
  a Alfred pretends he doesn't understand what Mr. Carr is thinking.
  b Alfred is insulted that Mr. Carr thinks he is a thief.
  c Alfred hopes Mr. Carr will think he's scared.

2 Alfred asks Mr. Carr, "Do you have to tell her?"
  a Alfred wants Mr. Carr to call the police instead of his mother.
  b Alfred knows his mother isn't at home.
  c Alfred is scared and hopes Mr. Carr will change his mind.

3 On the walk home, Alfred tells his mother, "That's the last time."
  a Alfred is telling his mother that he will not steal again.
  b Alfred is lying to his mother.
  c Alfred doesn't want to talk to his mother anymore.

4 Alfred says, "I'd like to tell her she was great with Mr. Carr."
  a Alfred wants his mother to feel proud of him.
  b Alfred respects the way his mother behaved with Mr. Carr.
  c Alfred likes Mr. Carr.

3 Analyzing the Story: Tone

As you read on page 156, tone shows the writer's feelings about the subject and characters. The writer sets the tone through description and dialogue. Three types of tone from the story are in the chart. Examples of descriptions or dialogue are shown for each type of tone. Read the story again and look for more examples to add to the chart.

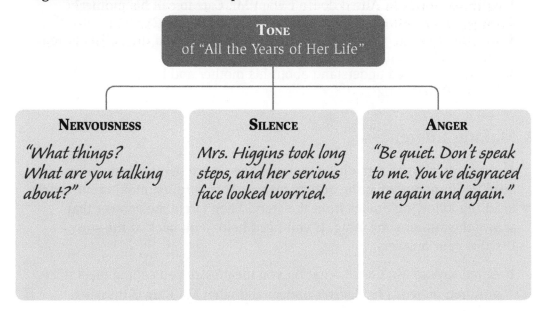

TONE
of "All the Years of Her Life"

NERVOUSNESS	SILENCE	ANGER
"What things? What are you talking about?"	*Mrs. Higgins took long steps, and her serious face looked worried.*	*"Be quiet. Don't speak to me. You've disgraced me again and again."*

4 Summarizing

Put the following sentences in the correct order to summarize the story. Write the numbers 1 to 6 to show the order. The first one has been done for you.

____ Mr. Carr calls Mrs. Higgins on the telephone.

____ Alfred and his mother walk home in silence.

_1_ Mr. Carr accuses Alfred of stealing from the store.

____ Mrs. Higgins is calm and dignified in the store.

____ Mr. Carr agrees not to call the police.

____ Alfred watches his mother drink the tea with a trembling hand.

5 Writing

Pretend you are Alfred. Write a letter to Mr. Carr. Explain how sorry you are about stealing from him and about the lesson you learned.

A TAKE A CLOSER LOOK

1 Theme Comparison: Close Relationships

The three stories in Part Four describe the happiness, disappointment, secrets, and conflicts the characters have with each other. They also describe the knowledge the characters gain about themselves and about each other. Pan discovers who she is and learns the meaning of betrayal. Peter Brench understands that he does not want to accept the truth of his secrets. Alfred realizes the pain he has caused his mother.

With a partner, discuss the following questions:

1 How does Mark destroy his close relationship with Pan?
2 In what ways does Peter prove to be a good friend to the Mallows?
3 How do you think Mrs. Higgins feels about her son and about her life?

2 Freewriting

Write the words *close relationships* at the top of a sheet of paper. Then write any words that come into your mind when you think of close relationships. For 15 minutes, write about the close relationships in your life. Who are the people closest to you? How do they make you feel? What have you learned from them? Have they ever disappointed you? Have you ever disappointed them?

B REVIEW

1 Grammar Review

Connect the following pairs of sentences to create a one-paragraph summary of the three stories in Part Four. Use the conjunctions and transitions in Chapter 11.

The characters in Part Four had conflicts. There was also love in their
    relationships.
Pan was betrayed by Mark. He expected Pan to love him.
Mrs. Mallow loved her husband. She pretended his art was good.
Alfred was proud of his mother. He was amazed at her dignity.

2 Vocabulary Review

The definitions under *Across* and *Down* are for vocabulary words in Part Four. Read the definitions and complete the crossword puzzle with the correct vocabulary words.

Across
2 practices or habits of a person, group, or country
5 find bad things about someone or something
7 say or think that someone is responsible for something bad that happened
8 prevent someone or thing from being hurt
10 give someone hope; tell someone to keep trying
12 well-known by many people
14 annoy

Down
1 concerned about a problem or something about to happen
3 sign that is used to represent something else
4 shaky; thinking about something about to happen, like a test
5 find the similarities or sameness between two things
6 quick intelligence or problem solving
9 relaxed
11 when the police take a person and put him or her in jail
13 good judgment

C ELEMENTS OF A SHORT STORY

Filling Out the Elements Chart

This chart shows the five basic elements of a short story. You can find definitions for these elements on page 170. Some of these elements have been filled out for "Its Wavering Image." Complete the chart. Then copy the blank chart on page xvi and fill it out for "The Tree of Knowledge" or "All the Years of Her Life" or for both stories. Share your charts with a partner or in a small group.

Elements of _____ *Its Wavering Image* _____
(name of story)

SETTING
Chinatown in Montreal, Canada

CHARACTERS
Pan, Man Yu, Mark Carson

PLOT

CONFLICT

THEME(s)

WEBQUEST

Find more information about the topics in Part Four by going on the Internet. Go to www.cambridge.org/discoveringfiction/wq and follow the instructions for doing a WebQuest. Have fun. Enjoy the quest!

APPENDIX

LITERARY TERMS

Atmosphere The feelings or mood of a story are called the atmosphere.

Characters The people in a story are called the characters. The most important people in a story are the main characters. Other people in the story are minor characters.

Conflict Within a plot there is often a conflict, or struggle. The conflict can be between characters, between a character and the environment, or within a character's mind.

Foreshadowing The hints and clues that an author puts in a story to prepare you for what is going to happen in the story are called foreshadowing.

Irony In literature, irony is when there is a difference between what is expected and what actually happens.

Local Color Anything in a story that helps give readers a clear picture of what the life and times of the story were like is called the local color.

Plot The plot is the events that happen from the beginning of a story to the end.

Sensory Details An author gives you sensory details to create images of the five senses – touch, taste, smell, sight, and sound. These help describe a story.

Setting The setting is the time and the place of a story.

Surprise Ending A surprise ending is a sudden or unexpected ending.

Theme A story's theme is the main idea of the plot. Sometimes a story has several themes.

Tone The tone shows the writer's feelings about the subject and characters of a story. The tone may be happy or sad, calm or angry, funny or serious.

Vocabulary

The following list is the vocabulary from the activities in this book. The items are listed in their dictionary forms. Chapter numbers are next to each item.

Words

addition 3
adventure 1
amazed 2
angry 6
anniversary 7
approach 5
arrest 12
assignment 1
attract 10
awaken 5
balance 3
bargain 2
behavior 6
belief 10
belong 10
betray 10
blame 10
blush 2
boast 9
borrow 9
bow 2
bury 4
calm 12
carriage 5
casket 4
celebrate 7
cemetery 4
change 2
character 5
charming 5
clever 10
comfort 10
communicate 6
compare 11
confident 12
console 8
content 1
cottage 7
couple 6
courage 6
coward 6

cozy 7
create 11
criticize 11
custom 10
deceased 3
decorate 7
degree 1
detail 3
dignified 12
disappearance 7
disappointed 7
discourage 11
disgrace 12
distance 6
disturb 12
dream 1
drunk 5
editor 10
encourage 11
energy 6
enthusiasm 11
ethnicity 10
eventually 8
evil 5
expect 7
failure 11
famous 11
floral 7
foolish 5
forecast 8
foreign 10
fortune 3
funeral 4
generous 2
ghost 9
gloomy 8
grade 1
habit 1
handsome 5
haunt 9
heir 3

human 7
inherit 3
innocent 5
insult 12
interrupt 3
invest 3
invite 7
jail 12
jealous 9
joke 3
journalist 10
joy 11
judge 11
kindness 12
knowledge 1
lawyer 3
lean 2
leave 3
letter 7
literature 1
log cabin 7
lonely 1
loose 9
luxury 2
manners 9
master 11
miracle 1
mourners 4
mysterious 9
narrow 6
nervous 12
nod 5
nonsense 6
novelty 8
obey 6
ominously 8
pace 6
painter 11
passenger 5
passion 6
pillow 5

pleasant 2
politely 3
practical 2
pretend 6
pride 2
promise 10
protect 11
pumpkin 9
realize 1
reduce 2
reflection 10
remind 3
rob 12
saddle 9
sale 2
save 2
scarf 7
scholar 1
sculptor 11
sculpture 11
search 9
secret 1
sense 12
seriously 3
sigh 12
sleepy 5
smile 6
soldier 9
soul 1
spoil 1
stare 1, 2
steal 1
strange 1
stuff 12
success 11
superstitious 9
surprised 12
swallow 12
symbol 10
tale 9
talent 11

tap 12
taste 7
tear 7
tension 8
terrible 11
thief 12
thunder 9
towel 7

treasure 2
tremble 12
trusted 10
truth 11
tuition 11
unaware 5
unselfishly 3
valley 9

wailed 8
wallet 2
warning 6
washstand 7
waver 10
wealthy 8
welcome 10
whistle 3

will 3
wish 2
wonderful 11
worried 10
wrap 12
yawn 1

IDIOMS AND EXPRESSIONS

at home with 10
be worth 3
better days 2
board a train 1
break up 9
business as usual 6
called up 8
catch red-handed 12
catch up (with s/o) 6
catch your breath 12
check your watch 7
come to light 11
come to the rescue 6
deal openly 11
depend on 3
does for a living 8
don't fit in 1
Don't you dare! 10
drop by 7
facial feature 10
fall asleep 5
fall in love 6
feast on 9
feel sorry for someone 7
fill up on 8
fire someone 12
follow in someone's
  footsteps 11
get in trouble 12
get there in plenty of
  time 1

get tired of 1
go on stage 3
goose bumps 9
hale and hearty 4
hang around with 12
have in mind 5
have no right 10
head of 4
hold a job 12
hold hands 6
I'll bet you. 5
I'll take this. 2
I see. 11
just a moment 12
keep someone company 7
keep to themselves 8
lose its magic 1
made up my mind 4
make a living 5
make eyes at 6
marriage proposal 9
May I help you? 2
mouth watering 9
on foot 5
on sale 2
out of sight 5
pass an exam 1
pay attention to 3
pinching a penny 4
piped up 8
play tricks on (someone) 9

put him in his place 4
reason with 11
run away together 6
scrimping and saving 4
sell one's soul 10
send regards 7
(a) shady spot 5
show off 6
shy away from 10
sicken on the spot 8
sleep soundly 5
sprung up 8
sun goes down 1
take a nap 5
take a seat 2
take it or leave it 4
take off (leave quickly –
  depart) 6
take turns 7
Thank goodness! 12
turn green 8
turn white 3
wake up 5
walk arm in arm 1
watch every penny 2
(a) woman's touch 7
word got around 4
world revolves around
  someone 11
would rather 10
Would you mind? 3

ACKNOWLEDGMENTS

The 12 short stories in *Discovering Fiction, An Introduction*, have been adapted from the originals. You can find the originals in the following publications.

"Young Man Axelbrod" by Sinclair Lewis, from *Selected Short Stories of Sinclair Lewis*. Published by Doubleday, Doran, Garden City, New York, 1935.

"A Pair of Silk Stockings" by Kate Chopin, from *Bayou Folk*. Published by Houghton Mifflin & Co., Boston and New York, 1894.

"One Thousand Dollars" by O. Henry, from *Introducing the Short Story*, edited by Christ and Shostak. Published by Masco Publications, Inc., New York, 1991.

"Omit Flowers" by Dana Burnet. Copyright © 1931 by P.F. Collier and Son Company.

"David Swan" by Nathaniel Hawthorne, from *Twice Told Tales*. Published by Maynard, Merrill & Co., New York, 1897. First published in *The Token and Atlantic Souvenir*, Boston, 1837.

"The Pace of Youth" by Stephen Crane, from *Great Short Works of Stephen Crane*. Published by Perennial Press (a HarperCollins publication), New York, 2004. First published in the *New York Press*, New York, January 1895.

"The Californian's Tale" by Mark Twain. First published in *Harper's Magazine*, New York, 1902.

"Rain, Rain, Go Away" by Isaac Asimov, from *Buy Jupiter and Other Stories* by Isaac Asimov, copyright © 1975 by Isaac Asimov. Used by permission of Doubleday, a division of Random House, Inc. and reprinted by permission of the Estate of Isaac Asimov.

"The Legend of Sleepy Hollow" by Washington Irving, from *The Complete Tales of Washington Irving*. Published by Doubleday & Co., Garden City, New York, 1975.

"Its Wavering Image" by Edith Eaton, from *Mrs. Spring Fragrance and Other Writings*, edited by Amy Ling and Annette White-Parks. Published by University of Illinois Press, 1995.

"The Tree of Knowledge" by Henry James, from *The Best Short Stories of the Modern Age* by Douglas Angus. Published by Ballantine, New York, 1987.

"All the Years of Her Life" by Morley Callaghan, appears in *The Complete Stories, Volume One*, by Morley Callaghan, pages 1–8, published by Exile Editions, © 2003.

The authors would like to thank the following reviewers for their thoughtful and useful feedback: Guillermo Colls, Cuyamaca College, El Cajon, California; Mary Corredor, Austin Community College, Austin, Texas; Margaret Edwards, Miami Dade Community College, Miami, Florida; and Susan Thompson, Norwalk Community College, Norwalk, Connecticut.

INDEX